What others are saying about

"Kyczy Hawk is a gifted spiritual teacher who generously shares her journey with candidness and humility. In *"Life in Bite-Sized Morsels"* Kyczy writes with a practical voice that makes you feel like you're sitting across from her having tea or hanging out with her at the studio. The format of this beautiful collection is appropriate for both newcomers to yoga and those with many years of practice...there is something for everyone here. This book serves as an important contribution to the evolution of recovery yoga!"

-Jamie Marich, Ph.D., LPCC-S, LICDC-CS
Founder of Dancing Mindfulness
Author, *"Trauma and the Twelve Steps"*, *"Trauma Made Simple"*, *"EMDR Made Simple"*, and *"Dancing Mindfulness"*

""*Life in Bite-Sized Morsels*" has already earned a special place in my favorite reading spot next to my most treasured morning meditation books. Kyczy Hawk has a talent for taking the feelings that go along with the experiences of being human and putting them into words. Her passion and gift for sharing the message of recovery has inspired me in every way imaginable. The writings of this beautifully honest teacher continue to mentor my heart from afar."

-Marta Mrotek; talented yoga teacher and Author of *"Miracle in Progress"* and *"Miracle in Progress Workbook: A Workbook for Holistic Recovery "*

"Kyczy Hawk has written a gift in *"Life In Bite-Sized Morsels"* - not only for those in recovery from both sides of this family disease - but for anyone wanting to embark on and along the way, live, their "journey to becoming genuine." Kyczy shares her journey from places so deep and vulnerable - places you'll recognize and rejoice in her having given them voice - for it's her humanness, questing spiritedness, compassion, honesty and humility that come through on every page make it safe to believe you, too, can start or pick up where you left off. This is one book you'll want to read multiple times. "

-Lisa Frederickson - author of nine books, including "Secondhand Drinking" and "Quick Guide to Addiction Recovery: What Helps, What Doesn't". Lisa is a nationally recognized speaker on women's history, addiction, and recovery.

"If you ever feel you are alone in your feelings or in your fight to remain calm and steady in the turbulent waters of life, just pick up a copy of Kyczy Hawk's latest offering, "Life in Bite-Sized Morsels". Her compassion and her honesty both contribute to this unique and inspiring view of life. This is a book you will want to keep in a handy spot on your shelf and read over and over again.

-Meridith Berk, Writer and Researcher "Antidepressants: What Every Patient Needs to Know"

"Life in Bite-Size Morsels" is a delightful book where author Kyczy Hawk shares her insights about life, long-term recovery, the 12- Steps, meditation as well as the incredible value of yoga. The book is well written and in an easy format to read one section at a time.

This book is filled with passion, empathy and understanding for anyone journeying down the recovery path or looking for wise perceptions about life. Through Kyczy's experiences, the reader can learn the importance of letting go of busyness, coping with loss, gratitude, love, forgiveness and more. I would highly recommend this book to anyone on the recovery journey or anyone interested in getting at the heart of living a more aware life."

-Cathy Taughinbaugh, Certified Parent Coach, Life Coach and Life and Recovery Coach and she works with the Parent Support Network for the Partnership for Drug-Free Kids

Life In Bite-Sized Morsels

Life In Bite-Sized Morsels

Learning to Live "Life on Life's Terms"*

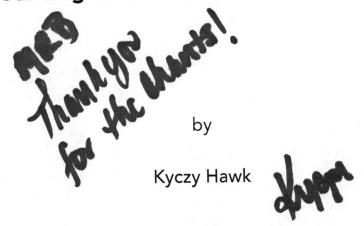

by

Kyczy Hawk

(*A phrase attributed to many, from Charles M. Schulz to Chris Farley.)

ISBN: 1511946792
ISBN 13: 9781511946797
Library of Congress Control Number: 2015906838
CreateSpace Independent Publishing Platform
North Charleston, South Carolina

Dedication

To Leslie Hagen, wise beyond her years, compassionate beyond limits, and funny without remorse. Thank you for your wit and wisdom in sharing with our Y12SR group. We hold you dear.

Table of Contents

Acknowledgements

"Life in Bite-Sized Morsels"

PROFESSIONAL FEEDBACK, MENTORING and guidance brought this from blog to book. Thank you Eileen Brewer, Meridith Berk and my new editor pal Todd Larson. You gave me feedback and encouragement cleaning up my initial scattered writings to a cohesive set of entries.

The faithful members of the San Jose posse of Y12SR (Yoga of 12 Step Recovery) groups listened to me patiently as I worked through these issues; the topics that were to make themselves into my writing. Thank you to Willow Glen Yoga for giving us space. We meet together at least once a week, listen and support one another as we investigate living "life on life's terms". We come to grips with new ways to address our difficulties. We use our yoga in the discussion and on the mat, finding new peace and depth to being people in recovery. Thank you.

I have a home group; "In The Solution" in San Jose CA Saturday mornings. The members celebrate the joy in life with me and hold me up when I am down. They encourage me with unwavering affection and help me believe what is good about myself. I am so blessed.

A special thanks to the Addiction and Related Topics group. For one full year we each read and gave feedback on one another's blogs and articles. They encouraged me to continue writing, They allowed me to struggle in my journey while offering me safe shore when I needed it.

Scattered across the US the internet allowed this kind of support to be possible. In particular thank you Lisa Frederiksen, Cathy Taughinbaugh, Bill White, Beth Wilson and Jody Lamb. I always feel honored to be in your tribe.

Family! My greatest opportunity for both challenge and for healing. All generations in all directions of relations, thank you; I am grateful. A particular hug to Meridith Berk, an author in her own right, for loving me and loving my writing. Thank you sis for "hanging out" during recess, laughing together and helping me to remember that this is supposed to be fun.

A huge bow of deep gratitude to Rick Snively who provided the images for this book. His love of Elkhorn Slough, a neighboring marshland, shows through in these photographs and in his love of nature overall. He shares his vision and artwork in books and framed pieces.

Finally I want to acknowledge the people who have written me to tell me that they have felt the same, that my words have reminded them of similar experiences, that what I have written had helped them in some way. That is a huge honor, to be part of someones' ease. A thought, a memory or a breath, let loose and re-integrated; sharing through writing is a grace. I thank you for letting me know.

Introduction

I AM A woman in long-term recovery. I do not take my recovery for granted, but day by day I take greater comfort and security in it. My consistent holding of Yoga of 12-Step Recovery (Y12SR) meetings and working with others in their recovery processes keeps my program fresh. I continually work the steps on any issue that crops up that may hamper my enjoyment of life or of others in my life. I still retain "leftovers" from my growing-up years and from my disease. I am not free of them, only more skilled at confronting them and making peace with them.

Whether you are in recovery or just an alert participant in your life, your life offers you gigantic helpings of both the enjoyable and the difficult at seemingly random times. A surprise visit from an old friend, a new job, a new career opportunity, and the addition of a family member through marriage or birth are all good things, but they can still rock you off balance. An accident, an illness, aging, and the death of someone dear to you can shift your outlook on life. Changes like these will prompt reevaluation and introspection. This is natural.

Ashleigh Brilliant published a book in 1987 titled *I Try to Take One Day at a Time, but Sometimes Several Days Attack Me at Once.* That is as funny as it is true. Usually my days occur one at a time, but sometimes they have treated me to challenging events. Yet I have the resources to meet them, so I can deal with "life on life's terms." I have trusted people to call, self-care techniques, favorite meetings, meditation practice, and, of course, yoga. I have sufficient tools so that if I forget about one, I have others at hand. Even when life comes at me all at once, I have ways of grounding myself.

Yet sometimes a small, seemingly insignificant event can rock your world—choosing a watch band, contracting laryngitis, continuing to develop healthy self-love—nothing earth shattering, but all capable of causing pause, disturbing equanimity, and possibly growing into an ethical inquiry or a reevaluation of prior assumptions. These are awakening moments—the stuff of life. Viktor E. Frankl writes in *Man's Search for Meaning*: "Thus suffering completely fills the human soul and conscious mind, no matter whether the suffering is great or little. Therefore the 'size' of human suffering is absolutely relative." He later mentions that even a hangnail can hold one's complete attention.

Many of these essays refer to the hangnails in life, the annoying and all-encompassing moments that have hijacked my attention and provoked me to consider things in a different light. I have learned to investigate them, to focus on one moment at a time, taking *life in bite-sized morsels*.

Yoga enables me to do this. Yoga has somatic (mind and body connection) benefits in addition to being a healthful physical practice and an ethical and philosophical journey. I had no idea that when I "stepped onto the mat" (yoga-speak for beginning a yoga practice) that I would be immersed in a physical practice that nourished and strengthened my body as well as a study that would enhance and inspire my recovery from addiction and codependency.

I first experienced yoga when I was falling apart from the inside out. I had been clean and sober for many years. I had been in therapy, and was confident I had worked through all of my past issues, so I left therapy and continued in active recovery to flourish on my own—which I did, for many years. I married. I watched my children meet their own challenges and find their mates. I started a career and found a measure of professional success. I continued to practice the principles of 12-Step recovery and stayed connected to my recovery community.

Business and busy-ness, however, overcame me. Thoughts, feelings, memories, and unresolved issues from my past sprang forth unbidden, and I was not sufficiently prepared to deal with them. Living in the world of the intellect and the rational inadequately addressed what was going on. I was concerned that I was losing my mind, and I was afraid I would use drugs and alcohol again. My codependent behavior had once again taken hold, and healthy actions and behaviors were slowly slipping away.

In the midst of my near-breakdown, I walked into a yoga studio and took my first live yoga class. Of course, I fell in love with my instructor. And I followed her from place to place. Her compassionate tone of voice and her way in and out of the poses were such a gracious invitation. I also expanded my samplings to other teachers and places as time and travel would allow. I was bewitched, enthralled and transported by my experiences on the mat. I was filled and unified by my physical exertions, learning to balance effort and ease as I felt my feelings. The full experience of emotions welling up was something new for me, something I could not wrap my mind around, for understanding feeling had previously been a "head trip," always about intellect and what I *thought* my heart would feel. The stories of my past had almost seemed to be in the third person—events happening to someone outside of myself. I *knew* what one should feel, I could talk about it, but could not internally sense it.

Frozen feelings are one of the signs of being an adult child of an alcoholic. Empathy is as well. So with my abilities to empathize and to think about what feelings COULD be I was able to convince myself I WAS feeling. Until I became so busy and so involved and so success oriented that I became exhausted and had no defense against actually feeling. And these emotions came out on the mat. I started the journey to becoming genuine.

The surprise to me as I investigated more about yoga, listening to the teachers and reading quotes and then books, the surprise to me was that this, the yoga philosophy was familiar to me. The principles and tenets, descriptions of illusions and suffering written about in the ancient yoga texts were just like those discussed in the literature of Alcoholics Anonymous (AA). It was like the program of recovery that I practiced. I was home.

Life In Bite-Sized Morsels

A few years later, giving up my busy job—the one that had defined me as "normal" and "successful"—I took the training to become a yoga teacher, with the goal of teaching yoga to people in recovery, and I have now done so for many years. My book *Yoga and the Twelve Step Path* and my later yoga teacher certification program "Success Over Addiction and Relapse (S.O.A.R.™)" came out of this change from professional woman to professional yoga teacher.

In the process of writing my first book I started a blog of occasional writings on the intersection between yoga, recovery and daily life, in which I asked these and other questions:

- How does this journey of recovery and practice of yoga work on a daily basis?
- How do I find yoga in recovery, and recovery in my yoga?
- How does this process manifest itself off the mat and out the door?
- How do I meet challenges with my relationships with my children, my husband, my friends and my family in a recovered way—a *yogic* way?

I have included selected pieces from this blog here. Some are re-written, some are as is, and others have been strung together to give them better context and meaning. (This was, after all, a blog, a set of ramblings extemporaneously commenting on my daily life.) I have added sections that put a larger framework around the blog entries, giving a more personal background to the general nature of some of them.

This has been a journey about living ethically, authentically, and according to values that recovery introduced to me and that yoga developed on all levels of my being. I am now able to transform on so many levels: physically, energetically, emotionally, in my character, and intellectually developing myself as a fully integrated spiritual being. These essays describe how I live and breathe, taking life in bite-sized morsels, one day at a time. Here they are: *Life in Bite-Sized Morsels*, a woman's journey to ordinary.

ETHICS, VALUES AND KARMA YOGA:
On the Road to Knowing Right from Not-Right

I HAVE FELT the friction between who I want to be and how I am behaving. I know the feeling of discord between my intentions and my actions. I have felt the pain of knowing that my words and deeds are at odds with my ethics and values. I experienced this in my active addiction, as well as in my early recovery. It happens from time to time—even now. Rather than the bold violations of my values such as stealing and lying, I now struggle with the subtleties of ethical bypass that may occur from time to time.

Living an ethical life required me to adopt certain codes of behavior. The Twelve-Step program offers guidance—a process to go through to determine what is in alignment with your values and with those of the group. Service, humility, willingness, honesty, and responsibility are a few. We look inward to find these; we practice them in our community.

Yoga brought more form and specificity to these values for me. The tenets of the *Yamas* and the *Niyamas* (Restraints and Observances) are similar to the principles behind the Twelve Steps. The *Yamas* are roughly translated as non-harming, non-lying, non-stealing, non-excess, and non-attachment. The *Niyamas* are cleanliness, contentment, discipline, self-study, and surrender. They are similar to the principles of the world's major religions and spiritual practices. In the familiarity of their meaning, they give me comfort.

When I first became clean and sober, I was satisfied with the broad brushstrokes of leading an ethical life. For example, I was as honest as I could be. I needed to feel safe, but I also needed to let go of secrets. The safer I felt, the more I could reveal and release. Yet, like the child's game of sorting balls by size by letting them fall through holes decreasing in diameter, my ability to see the finer and finer aspects of non-truth increased with time. I have worked through the Twelve Steps now a number of times from several perspectives, and each time, I have reviewed this selfsame life of mine with a finer and finer-toothed comb. The result has been my greater and greater understanding of honesty.

The *Yamas* and the *Niyamas* have set those teeth even closer together as I comb through issues in my life. At the same time, those principles add dimension to my investigation: I look at not only my actions and my speech, but also my thoughts. I don't berate myself for unlovely or un-useful thoughts; I merely work toward keeping my thoughts positive and in alignment with my ethics and values. I listen to my thoughts to become aware of what is going on behind the scenes of public persona and activities.

⁂

August 13: Yoga and the Value of Non-Harming

The first of the Raja Yoga 8 Limbs are the *Yamas*. The *Yamas* are "restraints"—five actions that, when avoided, will reduce suffering and bring you closer to your true self: non-violence, non-lying, non-stealing, non-excess, and non-possessiveness. Like the 12 Steps of recovery, the restraints, along with other rungs on the yoga path, can become parts of the principles you practice every day to improve your relations with yourself and others. The *Yamas* are practiced in thought, word and deed; that means you can find many opportunities to use them in your life. Subtle aspects of these restraints can be investigated as you become more aware of them in your life. Harmful thoughts can influence actions. Speech can be as violent and destructive as a fist. Both actions and in-actions can speak louder than words. Attention needs to be paid to all expressions of non-harming.

The first *Yama*, "Non-Violence," sounds pretty straightforward. As an addict to alcohol, drugs, tobacco, gambling, consuming, etc., making the decision to step away from the "object of our [over-]affection" is non-violence to ourselves and others. In abstinence and restraint, we are practicing nonviolence. In the AA program we say we "cease fighting everyone and everything." We cease harming ourselves, the ones we love, our pocketbooks, our sanity, our safety, and our health. However, we may still possess character defects that continue to cause us harm.

Using the steps of recovery I have found behaviors in myself that had become harmful: anger, distrust, impatience, perfectionism, resentment, and being judgmental. Some of these come out underhandedly or obtusely; others quite boldly. These aspects of myself can influence unwise or harmful speech, even if I commit no harmful physical action. It has been part of my journey to recognize when I am employing harmful character traits. Those traits, uncovered in my fourth step and revisited in my sixth and seventh steps, have influenced my actions and my words. My sponsors and mentors have guided me in facing my harmful habits. Aided by the strength of looking at myself honestly, I have made inroads into non-harming, thus connecting with others and myself in a healthy way.

In addition to non-harming in speech and action, there is thought—the privacy of my own mind. This mind can torture me and tear down semblances of self-esteem I had worked so hard to develop. One of the addict's most prevalent character traits—a lack of esteem—can result from negative thinking, a form of self-punishment and harm that has no purpose in a recovering life. Even in my thoughts I must learn to be kind, to think as well as act with forbearance and compassion.

Non-harming has a foundation in language—the words used inside my head, during self-talk or when self-referencing. When making a mistake, no longer can I refer to myself as "stupid" or a "total f–up." Phrases like "Good try," or "Better luck next time," would be far more helpful. This is how I learn to treat myself as I would a favorite niece or nephew, as a beloved child—with words of encouragement and kindness. So why not use kind speech inside and out? Speak to yourself as a fun-loving kid. If nothing else, it can be amusing, with no harm done. So—just for today—try non-harming. In thought, word and deed, work on your character in this loving way.

⊰∞⊱

October 29: Acceptance and Gratitude are the Bookends of Contentment (*Santosha*)

Being enough, having enough, living in gratitude for what is and for who I am—what a blissful feeling. Unfortunately, this feeling can be elusive. It slips through my fingers in a trice. I can begin the day with contentment, living in the moment and finding the abundance, the sufficiency in the *now*, and then, like a breeze from nowhere, dissatisfaction arises. When I speak with someone, I hear a tone of voice, I see an expression, and—because my ego mind is so strong and self-absorbed—I react. I react to a perceived response to *me* (because it is all about me). I find that belly gripping, that shortness of breath, the constriction of the heart and chest, and I dive into feelings of scarcity: there are scant resources, I am insufficient, I don't know enough, I am inadequate, etc., etc.

I must then speak strongly to myself to *stop* this foolishness and practice a little self-talk:

Release my shoulders.

Soften my face.

Bring the breath into the belly.

Take a physical and emotional inventory.

Am I OK physically? Yes—relax.

Am I OK emotionally? If not, why not?

What is the source of my discomfort? Illusion? Grasping? Avoidance? Find out what is going on, and attend to it.

Self-soothe. Let go of holding and expectation. Ask for help if needed, then notice I am OK.

What happens when I pull gratitude back into my heart? Ease.

I am complete in the moment.

After the frantic searching and a dance with dis-ease, I am, once again, content.

Santosha is the observance of contentment. Today I read from Deborah Adele's book, *The Yamas and the Niyamas*, that contentment is a state of being that requires attention as well as in-attention—a cosmic balance. I must be mindful, but not grasping to experience it.

We are encouraged into a state of longing by advertisers who constantly offer us new things or "new and improved" versions of what we already have. The scanning and seeking something different has been part of our genetic being for generations. We looked for movement in the bushes that could indicate a predator; our eyes jumped to a twig that could have been a snake. What once had kept us from harm by identifying the unusual has now been converted—or perverted—into scanning the horizon for something new, something I *need*, something I *want*, some desire previously unknown to me. This sense of being watchful and seeking the new has been transformed into longing, a desire now magnified by advertisers' efforts.

To counter these feelings of longing, I practice looking around and contemplating gratitude. I am grateful for that which I am, have and know *now*. As I think about this wanting and desiring, I also consider that possessions possess us, and "things" can often become a burden—golden handcuffs that bind us to our things, or even to our life circumstances.

I am learning to be content in the moment. It is a journey. At times I am still more involved and invested in *getting ready* to live rather than being, rather than to experience, to *exhale*, to be who I am; involved in the process of becoming rather than being. This is discontentment. Part of this discontent and outside referencing is the poisonous activity of comparison: comparing my outsides to another's, so that my home, my work, my goods, etc., pale in comparison to those aspects of someone else's life. I am never comforted when I compare myself to others: I emerge erroneously lacking or making negative judgments in order to "come out on top." Illusions of the false appearing real destroy the richness of the present moment. Envy and expectations rob the current moment from the fullness of its due. To come back to reality, I look to *gratitude* for what I have and who I am.

I also poison contentment by looking outside myself and expecting others to meet my needs, in effect looking to others for sustenance and completion. That action and view can only disappoint. I become emotionally disquieted and lose connection with my true self. To counter my "otheration," I look inward and find strength and gratitude.

Emotional disturbance can pull me out of contentment, while finding the root cause of that disturbance can help me gain insight into it, and finding compassion with this cause can move me closer to contentment than before. My ill feelings and ill will can be catching: I can poison all around me with the consequences of my negative behavior. And it happens fast. It can take the tick of the clock to give fear, resentment, anger or hurt to another. I need to go through my feelings to their source in order to redeem them, reform them, and reduce the risk of acting on them. Taking responsibility for the resolution to these out-of-balance feelings can start with gratitude for taking action when one should, and for *not* taking action when one shouldn't.

A key to this is accepting things as they are. Often I find myself grasping pleasure and avoiding pain, thereby creating discontent in myself by searching for something that is other than it is. Like the shaggy dog, I go to extreme lengths to find one thing and run away from the other, only to find that the pleasurable has a price and the pain is unavoidable. Moreover, the mere activity of running to or from exhausts and disturbs me. To find balance, find acceptance. In acceptance, find gratitude. Contentment for me comes from being the right size, doing enough, being enough, being grateful that all is as is should be. When I am here, in this place of calm, I can contribute to the sense of wellbeing all around me, with honesty and honor.

❦

April 5: The Yoga of Letting Go

Another *Yama* is *aparigraha*, or non-attachment. As yoga is an ancient wisdom and practice, attachment has been a problem for ages. We modern people are not exclusively vexed. The ancients were afflicted as much as we. Yoga provides strategies and teachings to guide us in letting go. Here are some steps we can follow to begin to release the death grip on things that cause us to suffer.

The first step in the process is to identify that to which we are holding on. The gripping can be at the emotional, intellectual, or even physical level—sometimes all three. Each time I encounter these feelings, I must reexamine where they are coming from, and I need to know what I am grasping before I can follow a path to release:

1. Is it an idea, such as a limitation? ("I can't do this or that," "They mustn't do this or that," "We should..." "They should..." and so on.)
2. Is it an activity like being online, checking and rechecking communication feeds to verify connections? Is it shopping and buying—looking for "something else" that will suit me, making me complete, or giving me the emotional lift a purchase can provide?
3. Could it be a behavior, such as exerting control over another, dictating and directing another's actions and activities? Is it meddling? Is it manipulation and passive manners of control?
4. Could it be a substance in which the overindulgence is causing internal conflict or disassociation? Could it be food where companionship is really being sought, where loneliness has set in? Or is it intoxicants polluting mind, body and spirit, softening edges and providing solitude?
5. Is it unhealthy companionship taking the place of self-affirmation, self-care and self-esteem? Is boundary-less love and enmeshment what you cling to, rather than healthy, balanced intimacy and relationships?

Holding on may be causing difficulties for you in several areas, some more problematic than others. So you would best focus your work on the areas in which the discord between holding on and letting go have come to an impasse and suffering is felt the most.

Your work begins by asking yourself, using the yogic practice of *svadhyaya* (self-study):

- Why do I fear letting go?
- What is the price of holding on?
- What is the price of letting go?
- How do I let go?
- What work is needed, and how do I do it?

Yoga is a practice. As we say in recovery, is it "practice, not perfection." This practice has several components nestled in the limbs of the royal path.

In addition to the *Yama* of *aparigraha* (letting go), the other *Yamas* offer guidance: non-harming, non-lying, non-stealing, as well as chastity or non-excess. By viewing your attachment through the lens of the *Yamas*, you can step through these ethics and apply them verily to each *Yama*.

Focusing on the ethic of non-harming, I can evaluate what I am thinking, feeling, saying and doing, and determine what harm exists in the thought, the sensations and impulses, the words and the actions. I evaluate the harm and make a decision at every level: the thought, the word, the action. Going through that process gives me an idea about the scope of the problem. For example, if I am uncomfortable about buying more things, I evaluate:

1. Am I harming myself, my family, my savings, and my financial security by purchasing yet another pair of black yoga pants, decorative item, lawn ornament, piece of jewelry, etc.?
2. Am I harming the environment by actively accumulating more stuff? What is the "footprint" of the goods, harm to environment

in creation, harm to people in the fabrication, harm to all in transport and distribution?

3. What aspect of myself am I avoiding by buying another thing?
4. Am I ignoring feelings of inadequacy or a sense of lack?
5. Am I trying to be or look like another person, thereby harming my own self-image with disdain?

Continuing the *Niyama* of *svadhyaya* (self-study), I can investigate the process. My identification of "buying" as an issue speaks to the truth that it is not a healthy activity for me. Moderation will be key. (Note: Other attachments, such as drug addiction, can only be addressed with full abstinence and other healing programs or modalities.)

Once my attachment is examined using non-harming, I can move to the next *Yama*, non-lying, to gain more understanding. I do so through the other restraint: non-greed. I examine the issue slowly and with compassion, not self-loathing. One can learn better with guidance than with condemnation. The lesson must be fully absorbed at all levels: physical, emotional, spiritual. It may require re-learning from time to time; such is the nature of being human.

What do I do? As the poses on the mat call for balance and investigation, so too do my behaviors. Some poses hurt me. My anatomy is not geared for that particular pose—perhaps only for a time, perhaps always. I practice the poses that give me more strength and flexibility and increase my endurance. I do this slowly, practicing the pose mindfully, or I may pay the consequences with injury—as in life: I face a situation, learn from it, and become more and more prepared for situations of increased difficulty. When I falter, I try again. With the guidance of teachers, interpreted by the sensations in my body, I adapt and grow.

I practice letting go of activities, harmful mindsets, and behaviors. I practice, I breathe, I look inside myself, I consult my higher power, and I ask for the support of teachers and others who may have already passed this way. I accept what is and work from there, setting my intention to accept change, again invoking the help of my spiritual guide, my higher power. I try, I readjust, and I try again.

There is no magic involved—only practice. Yoga has given us guideposts, and by utilizing them I manifest change.

⤛⤜

April 17: Anchors: Holding on and Letting Go

The British have a saying: "A change is as good as a rest." I did both by taking a vacation. Leaving home and my regular routine was refreshing and rejuvenating, but emotionally felt a little regressive. I have some engine inside that causes me to feel that a rest is a cop-out; that if I am "doing things right" I won't need a rest. At times, rest and perceived regression means a return to feelings, attitudes and behaviors that were there in active addiction and early recovery. There is an old tape that tells me that by letting go of routine and responsibilities that I am reverting to old behavior. How could being on vacation bring out the worst in me?

First off, let me tell you, I am in beautiful Hawaii—O'ahu, to be exact. Looking directly out of my window, I see the trade winds blow the puffy clouds across the sky. Gazing to my right, I see sailboats and surfers dot the ocean, waves roll up against the shore. This is my fourth day here, and the first that has not been filled with wonderful activities: snorkeling, hiking, sightseeing, walking and eating. Finally, I am at rest.

Yes, I am here in front of a screen, tapping on a keyboard; along with other daily habits, this is one of the disciplines I have been letting slide in my tour of paradise. Taking time to write and meditate has not been regular—my yoga practice is sporadic and the result of desperation (my muscles calling to me) rather than routine. Losing these anchors in my life leaves me feeling unmoored. The conventional markers in my day are gone. I can complain about habits and regular practices, but they provide comfort and can be the parentheses to my day.

While these vacation days are more full, with no predetermined breaks or pauses (except for meals), I am both strangely relieved and vaguely disoriented. This lack of structure is part of the splendor of vacation. Recalling my regular daily schedules, the usual demarcation of days beginning and ending, and the movement from day to day, I am both pleased and uncertain about being rid of them. It is hard to believe, for example, that this is Wednesday—I have lived a lifetime in four days, and no time at all has passed. Without the regularity of scheduled activities, time has changed shape.

A phrase from a book I read states, "No string, no flight," and this comes to mind time and time again that without some structure I cannot soar. It is up to me to reinvigorate moments of discipline in my day so that I may savor the freedom I have.

Renewed, I set a new intention to spend the time attending to those activities that provide the scaffolding on which the art of life is draped. *Aloha!*

February 12: Letting Things In While Letting Them Go

My heart is tender, yet greedy. She is sensitive, but grips tightly to what she desires. So strange to take captive what my heart admires as free. What am I doing? Why do I grip?

I admire everything that grows, and growth requires change. Pining for people relies on memory, which leaves me in a static position. Yearning for them in this way is just plain mean—and it flies in the face of what I believe. If I believe in change, growth and transformation, then why do I yearn for people and places to remain in a certain way?

I have children. They are grown. They have their own lives, and I love them for it. At this stage I no longer have a "vote" or say in what they do; their health and safety is their own concern. It is not my business how they construct their learning journey, what challenges and obstacles they choose, or how they decide to address them, but oh, how I make it my own suffering! I wish this, and I want that. My heart yearns for the details of their lives. I want these minutiae so my relationship can stay rich, so my close-ness to them doesn't slip away. I fear them becoming strangers—those who once had everything in common with me. I don't want to live a life of remembrance and memory, always bringing up the old stories of games played, meals shared, and comical situations that had become the fabric of our past. These things are important, but I want to increase the stories with the tales of *now*. This means *letting go* of the attachments to how things were and to allow them to develop into the sweet song of the present.

Clinging onto an image of myself, or my relationship with myself as a static thing, is also not useful. Some days I am on the beam-in the moment, listening well without judgment or expectation, listening to others and to myself. Other days, I resist. I resist the different, avoid change, and wrestle with reality. I do this with others and I do it to myself. When I continue to see myself in a negative light, I can hold onto this illusion and it thwarts and controls my actions. I become sway to this false way of seeing by comparing myself to others. Whether I find myself falling short or (rarely) finding myself more accomplished, the comparing always sets me apart. It is fantasy to entertain a desire to be a certain way. It, too, is static and smothering.

The trick is to *let things in* while *letting them go!* Enjoy family and friends, enjoy places and events, enjoy meals and music, enjoy my own age and stage in life. Let them be the way they *are* without comparing them to the way they used to be. Remain open to change, accepting dif-ferences, and allowing memory and actuality to morph and alter as they will: let one go to make space for the other.

⁂

February 24: Non-Excess, Desire and Cravings
It starts off small, a little *wanting*, a little attraction, and then a desire just this side of obsession. That is how it began for me.

My watchband had lost its loops, and the end of the strap kept flap-ping. It still functioned, but it was annoying. Then the band got a little tear. I was relieved. That meant the watchband was beginning to break, and I was in danger of losing the watch. Now I had a reason (and an excuse) to look for a replacement. This was where the trouble began.

Looking for bands brought me to the watch department, which presented a challenge. Nice watchbands cost $25 and above, but a new watch with band could be purchased for less than $20. What to do? The thrift of purchasing a new watch beckoned me. As I perused the cases, I became attracted to the dome-y crystal faces, the colors of the bezels, the feel of the weight, the variety of colors. Soon my wandering eyes had left the case of watchbands entirely, and I had strayed well away from the $20 watches into the land of absurdity.

Luckily, the high prices splashed like cold water on my face, the original mission became re-established, and I moved back to the first counter: *Watchbands!*

And money. I deliberated price: *Is my mission to strap a low-cost timepiece to my arm, to get a watchband, or to save money? Do I buy a watchband that costs more than a new watch and, by paying more, take a stand and refuse to add to the waste produced on this planet by reusing my workable watch? Or do I economize and get a new, sparkly watch to save the five dollars? Am I saving money, or the planet? Or do I need to save my mind?* Yikes!

Brain spin: Watchband...Money...Environment... I have many ways to practice excess: too much thinking, too many things, too many priorities. Yes, I want to "practice these principles in all my affairs," observing the *Niyamas*, following *brahmacharya* (non-excess). I want to maintain a modest environmental profile—not to waste what is still useful. I want to be modest in my spending—not to spend capriciously, but to get value for the price. Yet I want my watch to be useful in convenience as well as function. But I got so swirled up in the seduction of *new* and so wound up in the idea of *thrift*—where a new watch costs less than a watchband—and nearly violated my ethic of holding onto that which works rather than replacing it.

A lot of energy for just a watchband—but it is the way I process things. I go this way and that, breaking old patterns of thought and behavior, trying on different ideas to find the medium way. What comes first? Environment, or desire for the new and shiny? Thrift, or environment? Replace, or repair? What am I feeling? What are my enduring values? *Where is my breath?*

So what happened? I found the perfect band: not fancy, not elaborate—just like my yoga practice—but functional and just right for me. And it is *purple!* That was my playful indulgence…choosing a purple band. And I am best pleased. The *trip,* the process of discovery, was worth it.

⚬⚬⚬

September 15: Karma Yoga, The Yoga of Service

To participate fully in the joy and honor of service to others without judgment or desire for a reward or favor in return is crucial to my well being. For this activity brings me closer to people, and closer to the divinity in us all. I address this issue after my morning meditation setting my daily intention. I conclude my session by asking that all obstacles be removed so I can be of maximum service to others. I then contemplate the fact that when I am of service, I am not the "doer." I am a channel, a conduit, neither the beginning nor the end of the service action. This helps me to remember that I am not the outcome either, nor am I responsible for it. I am then able to be positively present with others and myself, not just to perform a service. I reiterate my desire to do so without an expectation. This is the meaning for me of "freely given."

In service, whether as part of my 12-Step program or based on what I discover on the mat and in my meditations, whatever I do needs to be approached with the right attitude. I also employ the action of the quality of *saucha* (purity). By keeping my side of the street clean, I keep my action clean of grasping or ego. I can be clean of ulterior motives when I perform my service, offer my care. Whatever I do needs to be with the right attitude, done in honesty within my capacity at this moment in my life, done to the best of my ability, and then let go. All I can take from it is learning from the activity all it has to offer.

This is a tall order! I often have an idea about what my "help" will do for others, what the service will look like, what it will accomplish, what the outcome will be. I am in danger when I say to myself, "I will do this so that..." for when I add a condition on the end of my thought, I no longer give freely, but with an anticipated outcome. That shifts my action from selfless service to a self-serving activity, even when my desired outcome is healthy, helpful, kind, or another good-hearted intention. Giving freely is not easy, and I am not successful at it all the time. I often do a service and "hope for the best." A service could be helping a newcomer adjust to new surroundings, being available for someone going through a difficult time, helping a person or a group to clean up, etc. It isn't straightening things out for someone or solving their problems for them.

Yet being of service does not have to be complicated; often the most simple of actions are of greatest value. The opportunity to offer help occurs almost every moment in life: smiling at a stranger you pass on the street, picking up a fallen object for someone, preparing a delicious and colorful meal for your family or housemates, etc. However, one's attitude and intention can move such actions from true karma to self-focused activities. When I offer assistance so that I will be acknowledged, my actions are not pure, not selfless. Therein lies the danger. To avoid that danger, I need to look inside, determine the actual reason for the action taken, and then choose the action.

When I step into a classroom or studio, when I step into or out of a 12-Step meeting or when I share a cup of tea with a sponsee, I must remember all of these practices: don't overstep, be where I am and be honest, and do not attach my ego to the results. Good class? Good meeting? That is not my doing. I want to contribute, and as a teacher I must lead, but I am not the message—just the messenger. This is how Karma Yoga and 12-Step work invite us into the very best we have to offer—to ourselves and to each other.

DREAMS AND DHARMA:
Awakening and Waking Up

————— ❧ —————

DHARMA MEANS "ENLIGHTENMENT" or "teachings." I certainly have received both from my recovery meetings, sponsors, formal presentations, workshops and talks. I have also received powerful messages from mini-awakenings, including dreams.

Lessons pop up from time to time as I wrestle with challenges and try to sort out what the true substance of the difficulty is. I often say, "A quarrel is never about what the quarrel is about—it is about something else."

In my waking hours I may get triggered or charged by another person, like my husband. Being angry with my spouse over a word choice and how painful it was is not about the word selection necessarily, but how I feel about it, what memories it evokes, and possibly some unresolved issue now making itself known. Taking the time and space to investigate the events and feelings can help me to wake up to what is really going on, work on my side of the street, and come back to the conversation and discuss what I discovered. I take the time to be enlightened, informed and educated, and to raise my consciousness about myself, us and our relationship.

This can happen with people outside the home as well—my feelings get hurt, or I read something that evokes historical emotions with hysterical reactions. I behave or respond in a way I later regret. But when I investigate the situation, looking at my side of the matter, I often discover deeper emotions, past memories, times when I had been hurt or fearful, and other feelings of insecurity that had leaked into the present time. Feelings and issues not previously addressed came out sideways in this particular event with this particular relationship. Other times I may determine the root cause or primary event, and it may disturb my sleep. While I can occasionally work these things out in my conscious mind, I often unpack the lesson in my dreams.

The following entries chronicle some dreams that were so important they evoked titles at the time, such as "Twisted Root Soup," "She Loves You," and "Being Guided Home." These titles were beacons of wisdom that have given me strength and reminded me of the course in life I wish to follow. Other dreams just brought to light in current dreamtime feelings and fears I had experienced in the past that I am now able to face. These events are not 4th Step issues, parts of "a fearless and thorough moral inventory," but memories that need to surface so triggers to past traumas can finally be neutralized. Finally there is an essay about how working on something in the present can open up old wounds that need to be debrided, once again to effect clean healing.

⸎

July 2: Dreams About My Mother

I woke up an hour after falling asleep, and dreaming about my family for the third or fourth night in a row. The last few dreams included Dad in unlikely situations, with unlikely roles. Tonight's dream had a foundation in what had really happened, but twisted, magnified, emphasized and enlarged certain aspects of that event to the point of surrealism.

In the dream, Mom had just come home from a rehab, the most recent of several treatments. Dad was thin, casually dressed, and appeared concerned, kind of like a TV dad, rather than the robustly shaped, seemingly disinterested man he actually was. I was a young teen, with a slightly younger brother. In reality, Mom would come home from treatment, get drunk, and get sent back to treatment, but in my dream, cops mysteriously appeared on the scene as she returned, held her elbow and led her away from the house, telling her that next time it would be the loony bin and she would be subjected to ECT (electro convulsive therapy).

DREAMS AND DHARMA: Awakening and Waking Up

So there it was—the day of her first furlough from her most recent lockup, and I was desperate to get the house cleaned up, though my brother and dad were not really helping. Dad looked exhausted and long-suffering, and brother was uninterested and distant. From evening to dark, I rushed around until the house was picked up but not quite clean. I was darting hither and yon to our many houseplants, trying to pick off the dead leaves and fronds, but the dry brown blades of the pygmy palm weren't yet dead enough to be removed easily, and they turned stringy in their resistance and frustrated me.

I looked over my shoulder to see blue and red lights strobing outside of the apartment window, following a car to the curb in front of the building. Up the cops came the cement stairs, the iron railings reverberated with each step.

Our front door opened, and police officers came in with Mom between them. She was holding a wide-mouthed beer bottle, smiling. "Do you know this woman?" one officer asked me. Suddenly I flew toward Mom, knocked her to the ground, slapped her with all my might, and shouted, "Do you know what they are going to do now, Mom? *Do you know what they are going to do???* They are going to lock you up and shock you, and we might not ever see you again!" I was so angry and disappointed that she couldn't even make it home without getting drunk, and I had spent all day neatening up the apartment to make her feel welcome...

Now my mother's voice took up the tale: "...and all I saw was a thousand ways they didn't need me. It would be six months and a car accident plowing me into the delta before I would step into these rooms." It was as if Mom were reciting her story from a podium at a 12-Step meeting.

Even recounting this change of voice, of perspective from child to adult, gives me chills. As the daughter who herself grew up to be an alcoholic Mom to wonderful children, a girl and a boy just a few years younger, in the dream I saw the story repeat and unfold.

Later I woke up and asked myself why I was having a "Mom dream" tonight. Yesterday I had spent all day with my daughter and just felt so full of love for her, watching our relationship change, pleased that I avoid meddling in her decisions and I trust her to her own way—in my thoughts and mind as well as speech and action. It gets better each time I see her.

I thought about how it had been for her to be with me as I changed direction in my life, what it had been like for her as I became sober. I also wondered what mom may have experienced not knowing how to deal with me as I fell into my disease and she grew into sobriety. I had been in charge when she was drinking. Who was SHE to ME when she got sober; who was I to her. She may have had similar difficulty in defining her relationship with me. I had been her caretaker all those years, yet when I was young and needed a mom, she was not available to me. Now, as a grown woman, what was was our relationship built on? I handled that by seeming to shrink to make room for her to appear "grown up": I didn't know how to be a grown woman with her when I later sobered up. She denied my alcoholism when I came to her as a young woman; even though she was pleased that I was sober. In a dance between acceptance and denial we managed a relationship from that point.

Soon thereafter, while still sober, she retreated into a series of illnesses. The more competent I became, the less she did. Was Mom simply making room for the only dynamic that she knew—big person/little person—as a way of giving up her sense of self so I could grow? Her notion that we didn't need her anymore since we had learned to survive without her was misconstrued, for living is more than survival. She also misinterpreted our trying to make her life easier by taking care of her home as "taking over" her role: the gift was not at all what she perceived to have been given, and what she had received would never have been the giver's choice.

Thus my new relationship of equality and respect with my daughter has no model. It is blooming on its own, and I wish with all my heart that I had had a similar one with my mom.

⚯

September 4: Flashback to Youth, Work Opens Old Wounds

A few weeks ago I was given the opportunity to contribute to a curriculum for teen girls. The focus of this six-week course for incarcerated young women is codependency and other fallouts from living in a house with addiction. Like Tooter Turtle in the Mr. Wizard cartoon, I have been time-traveling back to my childhood; to write words and present ideas in a form acceptable to a teenager, I needed to remember what it was like, what would have made sense to me, back then.

As a young girl, my life was chaotic. I didn't know that it could be different, but at a gut level I knew something was off. My home didn't resemble those in any of the books I read, the movies and TV shows I saw, or the stories of my friend's home life I had heard. In my occasional moments of clarity, when I found myself yearning for consistency and order, I heard some words of advice and care from unlikely places and people.

As a 12-year-old in boarding school (a catastrophic event in itself), I was taken under the wing of an elegant Indian teacher who seemed to understand my distress. I had no way to explain what was going on at home, but she bravely witnessed my confusion. When other events at the school made it impossible for me to continue there, she encouraged me to leave. I did, but not before she gave me the gift of her bracelet—"for strength"—right off of her wrist. This delicate piece of jewelry gave me a sense of being special, of strength through fragility. I have that bracelet to this day.

As a teenager I was "forced" to become part of a rap group (what "talking circles" were called in those days) at Planned Parenthood, one of the conditions of receiving birth control pills. We reluctantly attended these groups, as it was uncool to acquiesce with grace. What they offered me, in addition to some basics of health and choice, was a way to feel responsible. I was making a decision that was the result of responsibility in action. I felt worthy. The leaders let me know that life didn't have to be hard all the time. They could guide us. Since I had no guidance at home, this guidance was luxurious.

These occasions for help and support were as scarce as my opportunities to hear and comprehend them. I didn't have a lot of mentors or adult witnesses who were able to permeate the shell of misery that had been created as the result of being a child of an alcoholic. They were glimpses into moments where I could gain quiet support or calm guidance to help me navigate some of the perils of growing up when I had no other bulwark around.

I don't know if our current project can become such a voice for the young girls here at Juvenile Hall, but I want to try. It is worth the effort, even as the process of going back through time opens up vulnerabilities and accesses pain I thought I had long since resolved. I believe the work is that important. If even one girl can be helped, why wouldn't I help her? Difficult as it can be, I must continue on my journey into history and remember how I felt, what had helped me, and what I would have needed. I am reflecting on my past with the purpose of re-living having been a teenager in a similar situation so I can come up with guidance for the teens I am helping.

To increase my self-care through this process, I have been adding to my yoga practice, for half an hour a day over several weeks, somatic poses and TRE© (Trauma /Tension Releasing Exercises) designed to release held emotions. As I added these, I discovered more from my past to process. Though I don't have images or stories of the specific past events, I do feel as though I am detoxing, physically and emotionally.

My sleep patterns are strange: wide awake at night and desiring nothing but naps during the day. Yet I can curl up on my office floor any afternoon and float into a nourishing yoga *nidra* (not sleep) for half an hour with no preparation whatsoever!

I am a little cranky, I feel alternately unloved and then totally connected to the world, and I have hunger but no appetite—all signs that I am off balance emotionally, spiritually, physically and emotionally. So I redouble my efforts in all of the self-care I know and look for ways I don't yet know. But still I am un-moored and feel a little out of balance. Yet this is understandable: I am releasing even more from my tissues as I explore my teenage self, hoping to find valuable content to convert into the Juvenile Hall project. I was hoping for age-specific guidance to help me present a path to these young girls so they can hurt less and grow more.

Working out the issues and stories of my past, letting go of what is no longer useful to me, and becoming genuine is my *dharma*, my path. I am meant to take all of the resources available to me—my memories of rap groups, my counseling, my recovery meetings, my internal journey, and my external one—into my teaching and serve others with my greatest skill: listening.

November 30: Twisted Root Soup

My second child has been inconsolable since birth. He has the best laugh and a phenomenal sense of enjoyment of life, but gets disillusioned quickly and is often fraught with terrors: fear of change, fear of the unknown, wanting things to stay the same while remaining perpetually new. While he has learned a lot and mellowed some in his journey to become the man he is today, as a teenager this presented many challenges for him.

During those difficult years, I had a strangely prophetic dream about the dis-ease in my relationship with my son. In the dream he started out at eight or nine years old and later became younger—maybe two—as we were hiking down a trail in the woods. The trail's left side dropped off abruptly as the hillside fell away for twenty or more feet. The right side was against a hill rising about four feet up to another level of rough terrain. The trees were tall and dense; only a bit of sunlight strayed through the branches, proving there was a sun above.

As we walked and talked, the skies above darkened, and rain began to fall—first lightly, then in earnest. We would have to seek shelter until the storm passed. Tree roots were showing through the dirt wall on the right. They appeared to have been revealed when the path had been cut. As we sought shelter, I noticed soil washing away from behind the exposed roots, creating a little cave. With the rain continuing unabated, I decided to look for one of these crevices and take cover. (My son at this point grew younger and younger.)

I found a cave-let big enough for my son and me, and we crept in behind the roots and watched the rain pour down, lighten up, and pour again. My son became thirsty, so I captured rainwater to give him. Time passed. He became hungry. Having no food on me, I didn't know what to do. I looked at the roots and thought they must contain some nutrition. I broke off some little threads of roots and put them in rainwater. Voila! Soup! As it continued to rain and my son continued to be hungry, I made more and more soup for him—and began to notice something: as I clipped the roots, more grew. The roots twined at the point where I had broken bits off, and were growing more robust, and what had been a fringe of few were now forming bars of wood, creating a jail out of our sanctuary. I panicked—I had wanted only to nurture my son, and now we were captive! What had been a refuge was now restraining us!

I woke up with a beating heart, looked into the dream for meaning, and received the following revelation: "That which can cure, can kill." I cried. While I had been wanting to help my child and make "things easy" for him so he could be happy, I was, in fact, "killing" him by interfering with him finding his own way, developing his own solutions to life's challenges, and gaining the grit to live through being unhappy and find happiness on his own. While this was a huge wake up call—and a lesson in over-loving—I could not change my behavior completely. I made huge inroads, and I made big mistakes. It has taken me a long time to stop making soup, but I have. The occasional cup of rainwater will be shared, but not a lot, and not for long.

The gift I received from pulling back and letting my son find his own trail, his own path, is that we have become closer. He owns his journey; he is finding his own way. I have watched him become a man, become more confident, more self-assured, more responsible. Our relationship has improved and deepened as I let him be he and let me be me. A little bit of caring is appropriate, but caring so much that it puts us both in an emotional prison is not.

❧

November 30: She Loves You

I was a mess when I first sobered up. I stayed a mess for a while longer until I got clean as well. Even then, clean and sober, I could not disembark from my emotional rollercoaster. My brain wasn't firing right, and I had trouble making sense of life. I had a good automatic pilot: I fed the kids and kept a neat home, helped in their school, and got a job. I showed up on time to work and made it to recovery meetings regularly. My outside was looking "normal"—but *inside* I was pacing around in my ribcage, my feelings were huge, and I had no way to moderate them. Once the Pandora's box of responsibility for my past actions was opened in my fourth step, I could barely contain myself with all of my guilt and shame. In recovery meetings I had heard about tools for finding self-forgiveness. My sponsor helped as best she could, but I was embroiled in my negativity; nothing could get through for quite a while.

What cracked my heart open was a dream. I dreamed I was in a tall concrete structure. Since you can be outside and inside at the same time in dreams, I could see the building from a distance; it had the hourglass shape of a nuclear reactor. Inside it was nearly hollow, with a staircase spiraling up the walls to upper floors. Beneath the ground, trembling under my feet, a colossal engine with huge gears, pistons and steam rising from its block. I was turning this way and that, looking everywhere, trying to engage with my surroundings somehow. I heard a voice: "Kyczy, you have to slow down. Everything you are doing is making the engine work harder. If it [you] goes any faster, it will overheat and blow up!"

With that I noticed cracks shooting up the walls. The building was quaking and breaking up. The rumbling was deafening as I ran to the stairs and raced to the top, where a bit of light shone down through the top of the building. It rocked and swayed as the engine pumped faster.

I could barely keep my feet on the metal stairs, running up, clanging my way to the light.

Yet I made it. At the top was a little room with a little cot on the left and a small square window on the right. A sunbeam shone through the window and onto a form on the bed: wrapped up in a soft flannel blanket was a newborn, swaddled tightly with just the center of her face exposed. I felt panic as the building rocked and this innocent baby was unprotected. I grabbed her and cradled her against my hip. I positioned myself in the doorway, bracing for an earthquake, as any good California girl would do. Standing in the doorway with my feet apart and my right hand pressed into the doorframe making a large "X," I look down at the baby's face. A voice called out: "She doesn't know who you are, but she loves you very much."

At that moment I awoke in tears, hurting so much, yet feeling hope and a little bit of love. For the first time in my recovery, I believed things can change, I can be whole, and I am still worthy of love.

❦

December 4: Being Guided Home

I have vivid dreams. Many are merely sequences, stories, or entertaining events. Some, however, provide insight and guidance. These I make an effort to remember—including dreams about my death. I no longer find these frightening; I now realize they are about change, not my final "transition." I know change is coming, I have thought about my actions and activities, and I know a shift and realignment is due. I am uncomfortable, so the dreams help me work it out.

Last night's dream was about encouragement, grace, bravery, and receiving guidance. I dreamed I was in a small boat, like a canoe or a kayak, on my knees gazing toward shore. I was in the bay outside the harbor in Lisbon, Portugal. (Note that Lisbon is a sister city to San Francisco, also with seven hills and a bridge by the designer of the Golden Gate. The similarity is not lost on me, a long time Bay Area resident.) I was paddling in from the ocean toward land with my cupped hands, as I had no paddles. A passenger was in my boat, but I could not see him or her behind me; I was just aware of their presence. Even without the aid of the paddles, I was able to make headway kneeling in my boat, moving through the water with my hands.

The fog was rolling in. Within minutes, my sight of Lisbon was completely obscured. I had no idea where to head. I was frightened, but not panicked. My conscious brain was surprised by this reaction, while my dreaming brain accepted it. (This bifurcation of dream and "conscious mind" thoughts happen often in my "message" dreams. I feel what I am seeing, and see what I am feeling.)

The forwarder I went, the more lost I became. When on the verge of leaving dismay and finding fear, I looked deep into the fog, and in it were numbers—the latitude and longitude of my location—projected into the fog as a clock projects the time on a wall or ceiling. These numbers told me I merely had to keep moving in the direction of the appropriate latitude and longitude of my destination, and I would be guided home. Yes, this same fog that prevented me from seeing land made a perfect screen for my perfect pathway homeward. While in real life I don't know the map coordinates for any town, city, or neighborhood, in my dream the meaning of the numbers and the ability to understand them became mine.

As I paddled into shore and delivered my passenger safely, my resolve was to return to the ocean and use those guiding coordinates to guide others struggling to find the harbor.

I woke up knowing what my change was about: if I look carefully without panicking, I will find signs, signals and support to get me where I am meant to be. I need to get there under my own steam, using my own hands when paddling. I may have extra weight (perhaps the "old me" in the back of the boat?) or may feel on the verge of fear, but if I look up and around, I will find just what I need to see to help me home. And when I am ready, I can share this path with others.

❧

April 29: The Tiffany Tunnel of Life

I love language. I love words and their use. Sometimes my brain, however, takes the written word and weaves new applications, both reading and misreading a phrase. I recently enjoyed a mystery, *Still Life* by Louise Penny. A death occurs in the story, but the deeper mysteries that are investigated in it take place in the human heart. She writes so well, and her characters are true to life. She also does a beautiful job describing the venue: a small Canadian village. She described a lane lined with autumn-colored trees as a "Tiffany tunnel of light." How beautiful to combine the beauty of glass art with the art of nature to describe an image of light shining through colored trees like light radiating through a stained-glass window. I thought I had read it as "Tiffany tunnel of *life*," and realized, "Yes! That *is* what life is like—sometimes dark, sometimes light, beautiful around you if you care to look, but yes, dark and light. What a clever phrase!" Then I realized that my misinterpretation didn't make immediate sense in the context of the book (though it did, in a much broader analytical sense), so I corrected myself and read on...and yet, I couldn't shake the phrase "Tiffany tunnel of life." It blinked on and off in my mind, like a neon sign beckoning me to pay attention. Life has light and dark, translucence and opaqueness, these aspects shifting in time—life changes altering the dappled light. Sometimes the tunnel can be dark and foreboding, other times lit clearly in an inviting manner.

The mere reality that "the light" is changing can put one off balance. Busy days, hard days, disappointing and challenging events, even when punctuated with dinner and sleep, can be wearisome, and at times the world can seem uncaring, or even dangerous. The interior journey of working the steps or reconnecting with [unhealthy] friends or [difficult] family members can feel like walking from the light into the gloom. Old feelings come up, the trees close in overhead, the sunshine is blocked, the world goes dark, and it may feel as if it will always be that way. Yet, a few steps later, we step back into the daylight, and everything looks bright again...but even if you place yourself firmly in the sunshine to stand in that bit of radiance upon the ground, pining to be in that beam of brightness, the light itself does not stay. The earth moves, the sun sets, and you are in darkness once again.

There is no perfect way to stay in the light of the "Tiffany Tunnel." The only light we can be assured of is the one that glows from within.

MEDITATION AND THE BREATH: Looking Inside While Moving Outside

⟨~⟩

DEVELOPING A MEDITATION practice has been a big part of my recovery and an integral part of my yoga practice. It is difficult, it is easy, it takes only a short period of time each day, and it can take forever to get to it. Sometimes I sit comfortably and enjoy the journey, other times I feel like I am back in ninth-grade World History, watching the ratchet-tick of the clock as it inches to lunchtime. Listening to wiser, more seasoned meditation practitioners, I have discovered that that indeed is the experience.

Early in my sobriety, I had a sponsor named Shirley. She was stern yet kind, she was a group secretary, so she was "in service," and she meditated. She spoke about this at meetings, and I wanted to be with her, to be like her. I wanted what she had. I wanted to find a way to be in service, to have boundaries like hers. I wanted also to be kind, and I really, really, *really* wanted to learn how to meditate.

We read the steps at every recovery meeting I attended. We delved deeply into an understanding of the steps, devoting a week to each. I always listened attentively for the secrets of recovery meditation when we got to the 11th step. The words in the "12 and 12" ("Twelve Steps and Twelve Traditions" of AA) guided us but did not tell us exactly *how* to meditate. I was flummoxed. Do I close my eyes? Do I sit a certain way? Do I gaze at a candle? Can I use a verbal guide? What "counts" as meditation? How do I know if I'm doing it "right"? These questions would swirl around in my mind and became the content of my meditation time and time again. Despite Shirley's guidance, I was sure there was a right way and a wrong way to meditate, and whatever way I chose would be incorrect.

It has taken years for those ideas to be smashed. They reassemble at times and trouble me still, but I am a little more accustomed to the tricks my mind plays about meditation, so these moments of criticism and doubt don't last as long.

I had begun silent meditation with Shirley's guidance, but she moved away, leaving me to continue on my own. Subsequent sponsors had their own practices, but nothing definite, nothing of a specific form I could follow. I still needed step-by-step guidance; the practice still seemed so ephemeral. This was nearly 25 years ago, when the practices of mindfulness-based meditation were not well known and the Internet was not available to provide the now-available resources. Gratefully we had the "Each Day a New Beginning" and the "Twenty-four Hour a Day" books, but they were mere readings and contemplation. I wanted to *meditate,* to still my active mind.

Practicing yoga and becoming a yoga teacher has introduced me to many types of meditation. I can sit in silence, I can enjoy the soft sounds of nature, I can gaze at a candle, and I can be guided. I have learned that for me there is no One Way to move into the meditative state, as I have become comfortable with many meditation styles: sitting on a chair, kneeling on the floor, sitting on a cushion, even lying down. Being comfortable in a seated position for a period of time was uncomfortable to begin with, but I became accustomed to sitting straight and sitting still.

For a little over a year, my recently deceased sponsor Bonnie and I joined the *Dharma Punx* for weekly meditation practices led by Stephanie Tate. These were framed with dharma talks about recovery and the sufferings of addictions, and often ended with *metta,* Loving Kindness meditations. This specific meditation practice was, and remains, a huge help for me in practicing compassion and forgiveness of others and of self. Bonnie and I shared in our enjoyment of the group practice—another meditation method.

The other part of meditation that caused me consternation was the question whether I was "doing it right." How would I know if I were meditating properly? There were two sides to this question: *What was a correct form of meditation?* and *Why can't I stop thinking?* I had come to terms with the idea that meditation takes many forms.

I also wanted to understand my concern about the active mind. It turns out that the mind never stops imagining and ruminating, thinking, or thinking about thinking. That is the job of the miraculous mind. Meditation is the process of letting go of that activity over and over again. Sometimes naming the thoughts is useful: remembering, planning, planning for teaching, planning for travel, thinking about the past; noticing and naming the thoughts of the past we hold onto, memories, anticipation, and so on. Meditation involves looking at our thoughts and releasing our attachment to them. Another way to do this is to simply count the thoughts, number each one as it appears, accepting the idea that the thoughts will come and there are many. There are many ways to greet thoughts and release them. That is the practice of meditation.

There are also many styles of meditation and instructions on how to practice them on the Internet, in workshops, and in recovery meetings. The invitation is not "how" but "when"—when do you want to begin? Trying a practice and then trying another is a path into a daily discipline of meditation.

So how do I know if I am meditating properly? If it isn't the form that counts, and if I am not going to stop my mind from thinking, how do I know if I am even meditating? "The proof of the pudding is in the eating," meaning that I know I am meditating properly when I am not meditating, when the practice has been regular, and I am in my day. Am I more compassionate, centered and kind? Do I choose kinder words? Am I more conscious in my activities? Am I able to stay in the present moment? Am I redirecting or softening useless patterns of self-talk? Am I doing better in self-acceptance and acceptance of others? Am I more content in times of non-doing? These and many more can be signs of a healthy meditation practice.

❧

July 25: Meditation: Don't just do something—sit there!

For ten days I was using a guided meditation to refresh my morning practice. I discovered a useful intention-setting meditation: "Listening to Your Inner Voice" by Lori Leyden. It has had a positive effect on my days.

She begins by guiding you into a comfortable state of inner awareness based on safety and self-kindness. You are then encouraged to bring to mind a question you are struggling with, an issue you have with a person, or a decision you want to make. Accessing your inner knowing and trusting your internal wisdom, she guides you through the process of evaluating the questions and considering potential answers. It is very gentle and reassuring.

I had occasionally tried guided meditations in the past. While I benefit from all moments in meditation, some experiences linger. Leyden's practice has been one of those. It has helped me to sit still and process a current conundrum: my ongoing struggle with a challenge, reasoning and thinking and worrying this issue into the ground. Leyden's guidance, along with my desire to face my barriers and boundaries, was the perfect union with my practice. Sitting quietly, becoming conscious of my safety, and secure in my willingness to grow and feel differently, I was willing to shift along lines I could neither control nor predict. In my meditation, practicing *satya* and *aparigraha* to let the truth unfold slowly without constraint or control, I found my resolution, my new intention. I did not come to the cushion with a specific outcome in mind, but simply to sit in meditation with an openness to the possibility of change.

This is similar to my journey into sobriety. My only intention at first was to *stop it!* To stop the sickness, panic, chaos and uncontrollable mess that had become my life. I didn't want to feel the way I felt, be the way I was being, or think the way I was thinking. I wasn't sure how I wanted it to stop, but eventually I accepted that it would entail putting down the drink and drugs. That was as far as I got. I had no idea what would come next—so I just showed up, just as I had gone to the meditation cushion in later years to stop my rapid thinking and discovered that meditation was really about becoming open to life. I found safety in the rooms, I became honest, and I became willing. I learned to let go: to let go of who I was, and to let go of what I thought was going to happen. And my life got better, the future opened up, and while all situations have not been rosy, they have led to rosy moments and a life I could never have imagined.

Even now, when change is about to happen, I start by feeling lost. Then I remember I have to *stop it*, stop something in my life and let in something new. I stop holding on, cease grabbing, resign myself to the weightlessness of being between the bars of the trapezes, completely leaving one behind before making connection with the next. In letting go, I allow myself to be open to the intention of transformation. Being a newcomer implies a certain openness and a willingness to tread into uncharted territory. Practicing a specific type of meditation, such as "Listening To Your Inner Voice," means going someplace unknown with an uncertain outcome and result. It is like being a newcomer to my life. Each new situation, each new opportunity presents itself with a process of letting go, building trust and moving forward. I have jerks and pauses, and then cruise along with the smooth, deep breath. These become moments that allow my days to be beautiful.

⚬⚬

January 18: My Breath Is an Electronic Hostage

I have been on the computer a lot lately—for work, creativity, monthly accounting madness, professional correspondence, personal connections, and more. I have a laptop and a desktop. I have a new smartphone with all of the communication treats I had previously avoided—text-messaging, Internet access to e-mail, voicemail, etc.—in addition to the usual phone calls. I am now able to check multiple devices to conduct my business. I also check in to see if everyone still loves me (evidenced by replies or comments) on e-mail, Facebook, text, Twitter, voicemail, etc. Are people getting back to me? Are they initiating new informa- tion streams? Is it funny? Is it necessary? Do I need to respond? Am I in the loop with the funny stories, necessary information exchanges, general info, or just a BCC for goodness knows why? And on and on— checking and re-checking all devices, expecting each device to have new information.

What about the breath? In addition to getting "chair-behind," I am also aware of my inconsistent breathing. In anticipation of responses, waiting for a screen to refresh or a program to load, I hold my breath. I discovered this when hearing myself make an audible intake of breath after waiting for a screen to pop up. I have retained exhales, changing my expectancy to apprehension by starving my brain. No wonder I feel anxious when I work at the computer!

I remembered reading about this as a phenomenon from blogger Linda Stone. She wrote about "e-mail apnea" in 2009 and again in 2010: I sit down, open the email and stop breathing, day after day. As a profes- sional breather, I was hoping I would pay more attention to my breath and body, even when involved with electronics. Not so—I need to re- member to breathe.

I have the full syndrome: I experience computer-induced apnea. I have found myself holding my breath from time to time as I sit and wait, or sit and work. I have held my breath while scrolling through lists and scanning articles for salient points that would invite me to read them. I suspended my breath while proofing my own writing for grammar and spelling. Any time I was looking at a screen, my breathing would become erratic! I would hold my breath at the computer, phone or laptop. It was time for a change.

Becoming aware of this, I realized I needed to be more patient at the keyboard and to breathe with mindfulness. To help that process, I am cutting down on the opportunities to go astray. I have reduced the length of time I sit before a screen. I limit the number of inputs at a time (turn off FB while answering e-mail, close my browser when writing, turn off the phone when focusing on the screen, etc.) So far—even in this moment—I am able to stay aware, as I mindfully invite myself to breathe fully...and feel better.

To further assist me in remaining present and removing myself from the grip of anticipation, I am learning to let go of the electronics when I am with others. I am comfortable leaving my phone off. I dislike its interruption when I am with someone. Even in silent mode, the vibration on a table or in a pocket removes both (or all) of our attentions to the "Will she answer it or ignore it?" question. I feel we abandon one another until the answer becomes clear. We stop and wait—maybe holding our breath—until the sounds die or the device is answered, as if waiting to see if something else more important was coming and we were just killing time together until it arrived. This disrespects the present moment. (The secretary at a Maryland recovery meeting I used to attend would say, "Unless you are POTUS [President Of The United States] or an organ-donor, turn off your phone.") For now, for today, for my brain and body, and in consideration of others, I am practicing simplicity and cordiality, thus kindness—even in our electronic age.

⊱⊰

January 13: Meditation: Attachment and Aversion, Desire and Avoidance

When I sit in meditation, it is with the hope that I will...meditate! That I won't have thoughts that get stuck in the past or involved in detailed plans for the future. I am OK with occasional nuggets that pop up from time to time—it happens. Once the mind has settled, a lost notion or forgotten idea will pop up, but I place it to the side, hopefully to be retrieved later. And I return to the practice of letting go.

Those are the good days, when only a few unbidden items—images or words, actions or remembrances—float into the field of awareness, and I am grateful for that, as I am able to go back to the breath, the letting go of the desire, the attachment to nothingness, the aversion to anything. However, when I sit in meditation I often do have an agenda, a preference. I would like my meditation to be calm and void. I do know coming back to the breath 100 times is still "perfect." (Thank you, Stephanie Tate, for those words of kindness I take to my cushion every day.) But I admit I have desires.

So it came as quite a shock the other day to "hear" quite clearly: "With all that talking, you aren't letting your higher power get a word in edgewise!" That settled me down right-quick, as I realized that even the mental discussion about "It's OK, come back to the breath" and "Don't look to be in meditation, just sit and let it come" and all the other chatting I do about being on the cushion was a lot of noise that prevented me from listening.

But what am I learning from this message? I am seeing that ordering myself about in my mind (which, by the way, infects my daily attitude toward myself) is also too busy. And what are those wise words? "Note it and let it go." That is my practice now: not grasping for the nothingness, not avoiding the landscape of thoughts, but simply *noting* them.

❧

March 17: Just F*&^%NG Breathe

Yes, you read that right—just f-ing breathe. I was preparing to teach a Y12SR class at Elmwood Correctional Facility, where I go weekly to lead the discussion and the yoga class. As I moved the tables and chairs around, I felt some stomping on the metal ramp leading up to the trailer classroom. I overheard "M" advise other women to "just f*&@%ing breathe!" I was shocked, yet pleased that one student was advising others how to calm down. While raw and improper, the message was clear: breathe, and you won't be so upset.

When they came into the classroom, still talking and gesturing, I asked what was going on. A frustrating situation was happening in the jail: a change in snack offerings had upset some of the women, and a lot of negative energy was coursing through the unit (or "pod" as it was known). Two more women arrived in class about 10 minutes late as "M" was reporting the reason for the delay. Everyone was discussing the snack controversy; the situation was verging on lockdown. "M" and her friends had been able to leave the area and come to class, and the others, who were able to appear calm, were allowed to join as well. Once settled, we began.

"Just F*&@%ing BREATHE." What an honor to have the most vital lesson of our weekly Y12SR meetings be remembered and applied, at least by one of the women. She was using it, she was advising others accordingly, and she was able to walk away from an inflammatory situation without becoming embroiled in it. This goes to show how the breath can give you an option to act with dignity rather than impulsive anger, can help you think things through, and can give you perspective on a situation.

After the rest of the women filed in we talked about choices, dignity and breath, breathed together, and found peace. The class closed in calm. Quietly, with softer spirits, the women helped me to put the classroom back in order, and we left—they to their pods, and me to my life on the "outs."

That message about the usefulness of the breath permeated my life for several days to come. Later in the week I heard about the importance of the breath from a totally different source. I was driving and listening to the radio when I heard a man say, "We all just have to stop and take a breath." He was referring to the tar sands and pipelines and our rash decisions regarding energy. He knew, like "M," that we needed to breathe, step back, think, and consider the options, the sky and the land we are all a part of—not just for the present moment, but forever. *Take a breath.*

Sometimes it's OK if breathing is the only thing I do today. If my conscious thought could stay on my breath, it would be a rich thing indeed. I do have tasks and duties, things to do, and this and that, but sometimes it is OK just to breathe and take it all in—"it" being the *why* I do the tasks. Take the time to be on this planet with love and appreciation. It only takes a moment.

Pausing and breathing to disengage from a potentially volatile situation, before making a decision, or to gain perspective before running into a solution is useful for me. Taking a breath to come back to the present moment, to draw back from lurching into the future, to pull my thoughts and emotions from the past is useful as well. The breath is an all-purpose bestower of sanity, of health. Even in this moment I take time to breathe in and breathe out.

Once more, take a moment and breathe. Now. In love and appreciation. Then—off into your perfect day.

⌘

June 6: Start From Where You Are, Patiently

A few years ago I received a GPS unit as a holiday gift. Then it was a new gadget, sold before map programs were part of our ubiquitous smartphones. I am not someone who likes to drive, and even more, driving to new places can be overwhelming for me. The GPS was invented to simplify the process of going to new places. I still like looking at a map, but the GPS's instructions on a turn-by-turn basis have been helpful. They have taken some of the fear out of my travels. I enter my destination, and in a firm voice it advises me how to get there. I like it.

Yet as I turn on my GPS and wait to give it my destination, it takes quite a bit of time to warm up and load its information. I plug it in and wait while it takes its time to crank and churn. It pauses and displays dots and messages such as "Looking for a valid signal." Really! Are there lots of bogus signals bouncing around? Evidently. Initially this delay frustrated me, but now, while waiting for the signal to be identified and approved, I have learned to take time to think: Do *I* get bogus signals? Are all *my* signals valid? Do I jump into my vehicle and drive off pell-mell without consideration of my location or destination? Have I taken stock of where I am—where I *really* am, emotionally, intellectually and spiritually, before leaving to invade someone else's space? Whether I am headed to the post office or a friend's house, do I acknowledge where I *am* before I *go*? Can I pause and wait for a valid signal to identify the present moment and "location"?

After finally obtaining a valid signal, the unit waits and waits and waits until I let it know where I wish to go. It doesn't assume I am going to my prior endpoint, or the first location I ever programmed. It waits until I select my destination. I have to state, with intention, where I am planning to go. Even then, time is taken to choose the most direct route—not always the one I would have chosen—but, so far, a route that has successfully guided me to my destination.

In determining my own life path, have I considered traffic and intentions, route and motivation, speed and expectations? Have I found the clear avenue and taken my higher power with me all the way? I may need to be rerouted if the unexpected pops up, such as an accident or road-repair detour. I may hit hurdles or bumps in the road as I process my life goals. The illness or death of a friend or family member, a job change or new career opportunity, or the needs of someone dear may put a pause into other plans, causing me to "recalculate my route." Mindfully selecting my objective is a good plan, as is the ability to adjust my route while on the move.

While taking those few moments to let the gizmo figure out where we are, I figure out where *I* am. While waiting patiently while it plans the direction, I set my route with intention. I breathe while it calculates and displays, and I prepare myself for moving into the world with my total self in alignment. In taking this new view, I have reformed those morning moments of possible frustration into moments of reflection: where am I, where am I going, how will I get there, and how will I be when I get there? I contemplate not just the route, but also the integrated me. So I'm learning much from this card-sized device called the GPS.

RECOVERY AND YOGA:
A Powerful Blend Creating Strength, Balance and Flexibility On and Off the Mat

I NO LONGER introduce myself at meetings, "My name is Kyczy, and I am an alcoholic." I introduce myself as a woman *in long-term recovery*—often adding "from alcoholism, drug addiction and the family disease of codependency." I was first introduced to this new language "I am in long-term recovery" through the movie *The Anonymous People*. The message was powerful: *Claim your recovery at least as much as you claim your disease.*

I do not deny that I am an addict—I accept this to my core. But, due to my recovery, I am so much more. I am a full participating member of my community, my family, and my various professional and social networks. I am an author, a yogi, a teacher, and a potter. I cook and clean, read and rest. I sponsor women and provide and receive support from my friends. I have all of the trappings of a regular life: a car, a home, a yard, bills, and projects around the house. I never dreamed a life like this could be mine. Working the 12 steps, using outside help when I need it, and finding other life enhancing practices such as yoga and meditation have all contributed to my becoming a *woman in recovery.*

It is important for the brain to embrace the positive. Yet, again, it is critical for me never to forget that I have a fatal disease, which arrested as long as I don't drink or use drugs. The "stinkin' thinkin' " part took years to address, and relapse in this area is nearly as dangerous as a dram. To keep myself far from emotional relapse, I must stay in the active process of recovery at all times. I do recovery-oriented activities daily. I emphasize the positive to retrain my brain. When I go into the negative

("You are an alcoholic...") I am repeating the negative side of the coin to myself, which can lead back to a host of negative self talk—the very precursor for "stinkin' thinkin'." The other side of the coin is: Without my addiction, my alcoholism, or my identified co-addiction/codependency, I would not have recovery. Nor would I trade my recovery for anything. Recovery is a fabulous way to live.

It has been many years of "one day at a time" since I last used drugs in April 29, 1985. My last drink was even earlier: July 5, 1983. Which means I have had many consecutive days without inebriants, and I have had many days in a row to practice the acts of daily living: caring for myself and others, gaining self-respect, returning to school, finding a career, changing that career, and remaining an active, contributing member of my family. The difficulties, the pain, and the opportunities at this point in my recovery are far different from those in my earlier years of sobriety, when getting up and showing up on time, starting and completing laundry in the same week, eating healthy foods on a regular basis, stabilizing my moods and reactions, and relearning how to focus and read were all among my early challenges. I have a higher quality of pain now: aging, illness, death of family members and friends, and watching my kids face the adult adversities of their lives. There are now the fabric of my recovery.

That length of time in recovery doesn't mean I have had my head on straight all the time, but it does mean I have been able to notice "what condition my condition was in," to use Kenny Rogers' words. I have been able to reach out for help, accept it, and use it appropriately. In the past I had reached out for pity, consolation, and endorsement of my difficulties, chaos and pain when I was using drugs. Despite my friends' best efforts, I was not looking to change at that time, only to gain respite and comfort. In recovery, I have asked for and received help and have used that support and assistance to gain maturity, to grow. Now, when I am confronted with difficulties, I know I can reach for help. I know that whatever I experience is temporary. I know that if similar situations crop up, something in myself needs reevaluation and restoration.

RECOVERY AND YOGA: A Powerful Blend...

This is what presented itself over a decade ago. I was in emotional difficulty and facing the same feelings over and over again, dressed up in a variety of ways. I would overeat, over-exercise, and overwork. Exhaustion and anxiety became a new way for me to crowd out feelings and reduce intimacy with spouse, family and friends. It was addiction in a much more socially acceptable guise—but ultimately a way to "numb out." I was in danger, and I needed help. I found reintegration through Yoga. I also found a new calling in it.

Yoga has breathed new life into my recovery. I have found a philosophy that augments the principles of 12-Step recovery, a philosophy that gives me a life path and an additional way to work the steps. It has led me to a place to find deeper meditation, and it has allowed me to become friends with my body. Suffering and injury from the past stays lodged in the body, particularly when one does not have the skills to resolve them; yoga works this out. The arms and shoulders that would pulse with unexpressed rage are now strong and quiet. No anger remains stored in them. The belly and hips that were constantly contracted from past traumas and fear feel softer and more accepting. Knots that formed in my chest and ribs from anxiety and fear have lessened, and I can breathe more fully. My heart is lighter, and I have more compassion for myself and others. I still have some areas of tightness and discomfort; yoga is a practice, and it has taken me a lifetime to get to this point. It will take me some time to unravel it all. I now have an additional way to address the residual pain of addiction, of having grown up in an alcoholic and dysfunctional home, and of my co-addictive behaviors. I can refresh and release now.

We who work in the field of therapeutic yoga with cancer survivors, people with chronic pain, athletes, addicts, or combinations thereof all know yoga's benefits. Teachers who bring yoga into grade schools, secondary schools, colleges, universities, and remedial schools of many types understand that moving with breathwork and reintegrating somatically with the intention of just *being* is powerful stuff. Students have more focus, more impulse control, improved attention in class. Yoga is now being studied by standard researchers: evidence based studies are now in process, some have been completed. Studies involving yoga treatment for depression, anxiety disorder, back pain/chronic pain, cardiovascular disease, and cancer treatment have been done for the past decade. All indicate that further trials and studies are needed with more focused groups and specific yoga protocols, but the initial findings are huge.

Finding ways to apply these studies to addiction, prevention and relapse prevention is a stickier process. Long-term studies that include periodic follow-up are problematic. The empirical is limited to the subjective immediate response after a practice, but mid-term and long-term effects are less easy to trace and document. The population is mutable and mobile, and the follow-up on addiction treatment is paltry as it stands. Long-term yoga studies in regards to relapse prevention are difficult at best. It is also a challenge to obtain anything beyond empirical and subjective reports on the effects of a yoga session; no scientific reports on the long-term effects of a regular yoga practice are currently available. [There is, however, information about the increase in GABA in yoga practitioners [2007 http://online.liebertpub.com/doi/abs/10.1089/acm.2007.6338] and an increase in gray matter from a regular meditation practice [2012 http://www.hindawi.com/journals/ecam, 2012/821307/].) How closely related a meditative hatha yoga practice is to a regular seated meditation practice has not been established. If we had a longer, more thorough follow-up protocol with addicts in recovery, as already exists for cancer patients or diabetics, we could implement a standard yoga practice and follow its effects over a period of time. This would allow greater acceptability in the medical and complementary medicine communities. Insurance coverage of this non-western practice would likely follow, as it has for acupuncture, chiropractic, etc.

Even without the evidentiary data, we who practice and teach yoga know that yoga is beneficial to recovery. The ability to breathe deeply adds to the capacity to make good choices. The ability to locate and identify bodily sensations allows for more accurate identification of emotions, healthy movement, balance, and increased self-esteem. These are all areas of struggle for those newly in sobriety. They can be present for those of us who have been around for a while as well.

I am a woman in long-term recovery. That I have walked this road for some time means only that I have a different set of issues, challenges and problems than I had when I first became clean and sober. I also have a different set of graces, privileges and solutions than I had before. I share at 12-Step meetings that I have a "higher level" of pain, meaning that I now have more mature, adult type issues to address rather than the often self-made chaos of my pre-recovery and early recovery life. This is not to say that things don't happen to or around me, but that I seldom put myself in harm's way due to bad judgment and poor choices. I do that less often now.

Otto von Bismarck said, "There is a providence that protects idiots, drunkards and children..." and this was true for me. For all the times I drove impaired, my children, passersby and other drivers were spared. I did not get into a crash. I did not catch my house or myself on fire while freebasing. In fact I didn't get any of the terrible diseases one can contract through sharing needles. I was spared grievous bodily harm at the hands of abusive boyfriends and miraculously didn't lose my jobs. I was not kicked out of school, nor caught for stealing. In these ways and many more, Providence protected me until I could get clean and sober.

Now, in recovery, I deal with issues that are both more weighty and more nuanced. I am considering not only how I act, but also the sources of my behaviors. I am going back through time with a different lens, viewing my childhood and young adulthood with less criticism and more curiosity. I am seeking to understand how those experiences have influenced my life choices and am choosing now to make different ones.

A way into my feelings about these decisions and selections has been getting in touch with my body—my gut knowing. Through the effect of past traumas—some resulting from lifelong uncertainties, others from events—I had become disconnected from my feelings and my body. While I could sense intellectually (and almost sentimentally) how my emotions related to others, I was out of touch with them on a gut level. Then came yoga.

One outcome of approaching the third decade of recovery is that I am old—OK, *older*. That is both good and bad. While starting yoga in my late forties was so beneficial, even crucial, to my well-being, it was also hard. I have never been flexible. My strength did not involve finesse; it was more the product of self-will and brute force. I had learned to jog, with practice I could lift a fair amount of weight for my age, and I have the tenacity to stay with something even when it is uncomfortable. Yoga was uncomfortable, brute force didn't help, and my lack of flexibility meant I wasn't going to be one of those who "got it all" fast. I am smart, so I understood things easily at work and at school, but I couldn't get "good" at yoga rapidly. Then I learned that that is precisely the practice. The architecture of the pose needs to be sound, but the extreme shape is the result of anatomy, genetics, and sometimes youth. I learned more about what yoga was and was not over the years. I moved from a head-understanding to a body-understanding, and in that journey I discovered my integrated body. It was not integrated at first, but it gradually became integrated as I discovered the interrelation of my gut feelings and body sensations, my movement and my breath. It was terrifying, and it was glorious.

Yoga not only challenged my physical body, but also taught me ways to honor my sensations, feelings and poses. The different breathing techniques lifted my stale, still brain and allowed it a different way to process and shake things loose. Having a paradigm for meditation invited me to the practice rather than into a criticism of my practice—which was where I continually got stuck. And later, learning the philosophy of yoga, I was able to re-investigate the principles of recovery in a different light. Combining what I was learning about myself on the mat with the tools of recovery I learned in 12-Step meetings allowed me safe, speedy passage through another level of awakening and awareness: getting down to the *sources* of resentments, fears, anxieties, judgments and pre-judgments made about one's own capacities as well as those of others. The following essays reveal how yoga and recovery have been working together in my life.

～❦～

September 2: Who Is Your Teacher?

I was speaking with a friend the other day, and she boldly asked me that question: "Who is your teacher?" In our yoga practice we often have a steady teacher or style of yoga—a tradition that influences us. We may exclusively follow teachers of that tradition and may have a single teacher and mentor who guides our yoga practice and yoga teaching. My friend, an instructor, was talking about yoga, but I heard it at a deep fundamental level.

Who is my teacher? I ponder this question as it pertains to life in general, outside of my yoga practice. Many teachers and guides have helped me along the way. I have looked to other women in my recovery program to discern and design a new way of living. I have moved around the country quite a bit, so I have had quite a few sponsors, each one chosen at another stage of sobriety and having the unique qualities I needed at that time. I have also searched out people in the rooms of recovery who were looking to grow, blossom, and leaven their hearts and minds in a spiritual direction. My guides have not always been official sponsors, nor have they all been women. While I have lacked the continuity of a single person who has known me since the beginning, I have been fortunate to find "teachers" who were willing to catch up on my story and others who were content to address the *now* without knowing all of the *before*. My wisdom in following friends increased as my recovery matured.

Later, as a recovering woman moving into a career I have looked to others in my profession for guidance and support. Some were there in an official capacity—a professor, a counselor, and a yoga teacher. Later I found co-workers and bosses who were kind enough to give me the guidance I needed to thrive and prosper as a late arrival to my field.

Life In Bite-Sized Morsels

Perpetually open to advice and direction, I have remained an eager yoga student *and* leader—a wonderful balance.

A therapist I worked with for many years guided me with the gift of hearing myself out loud and supported me in finding wise solutions from within myself. I have thus developed enough faith in my judgment to make wise decisions when not in her office; she guided more than advised.

I received some profound lessons from people who had no idea they were sharing wisdom with me. With a simple word, phrase, caring look, or even a hurtful truth, they gave me just what I needed at the time to help me on my way. Sometimes they appeared as bad examples of actions and attitudes—behaviors to be avoided. Others popped into my life as good examples—ways of being I admired and wanted to emulate.

Peers are the most usual of my teachers—those who have seen me where I used to be and have shared a similar journey. They have been my friends in and out of the program who have witnessed my growth and have modeled what I might be, should I desire. This might be a typical situation for people who have "grown up" in 12-Step programs. We support one another through the process of growing up and recovering from our diseases; we show one another how to live life on life's terms.

I have also become a teacher and a contributor to my recovery community. By acquiring self-esteem through esteemable behavior, I can speak honestly about my own experiences. We all do that, hoping our experiences will provide example and guidance to someone else. I am also able to *hear* my own experience, listen to it, and work my way through the residual feelings my past has left in me. Thus I can see, from my own words, how I have changed.

What I don't have is a main yoga teacher, an individual professional mentor, or a single individual who guides me in my daily life. I have many I look up to, but in the course of my studies and my quest for enrichment and support, I have found no single source of wisdom. As a woman teaching in a developing field of yoga and recovery, new styles of teaching, types of information and types of student focus are appearing all the time. I cast my net wide and learn from many: Buddhists, mindfulness-based meditation teachers, yogis, and neurologists. I read philosophers and tap into social networking sites for people struggling with relapse and finding resources. I network with people in my field. All are my teachers, and all influence my work.

In the course of my work, I am alone for periods of time. I go into the treatment centers and institutions to teach yoga with my intentions in alignment and my heart open. I lead the class, and I move on. When I have taught and moved around for so long I feel isolated, my internal teacher reminds me to connect with others. So I *reach out*. I reach out to individuals among my groups of friends, professional and personal, teachers and students.

While the question "Who is your teacher?" initially filled me with fear and dread, I paused, took a breath, and realized that it was an opportunity to reevaluate myself and to be certain that I don't stop looking. This question can keep me open to new sources of support and information. Though I don't have a single yoga teacher, I have the capacity to learn from many and to be taught.

I don't have a single teacher; I have many; a mentor, a sponsor *and* a posse. These are all important relapse prevention tools, and I practice connecting with them daily. Possibly my journey is to weave together the wisdom of many into the guidance that is the truth for me.

March 6: Discovering Spring, Growth and Hope

I teach a yoga class at a place in the foothills of southwestern San Jose. We start at 9 a.m. This morning I took a pleasant post-rain drive up the hill to the center. While it is mostly an urban drive along a frontage road paralleling a major freeway, a pond with egrets, ducks and rushes is also along the side. A turn onto a side road continues the climb to the facility. As the road winds along the side of the hill, one can see cattle and calves in the higher ground, and wild turkeys and deer wandering the fields along the blacktop. With my windows rolled down I can hear the cheeps and chirps of birds over the hiss of my tires on the pavement. Flocks of birds fly up when I pass too close to a shrub that has provided them roost. Redwing blackbirds pose on the fence and the electrical wires that line the gullies on the side of the road.

I park at the side of the building, grab my chime and my mat, and close the door of my truck. A flock of wild turkeys complain and rush up the hill. The trees are in bloom, the sky is clear blue, and the breeze brings the scents of spring and hope. The spring growth is visible all around me—the newness born after a long winter.

I go into the hall, where the women wait for me on their mats. What joy it is to roll out my mat! I think about the long winter of active addiction as we move. Recovery offers a type of new growth emerging from winter's barren ground. In our practice we find grounding in our poses and healing in the practice. With hope we move into the spring of our recovery—awkward like the foals, needy like the chicks, and bold like the mother ducks protecting their young.

Roll out your mat, your dreams, anywhere, and *bloom*.

⁓

May 3: Using Yoga to Handle Fear: My Kayaking Experience

We recently vacationed in Hawaii with friends who had organized some wonderful day trips: snorkeling, beach walks, hikes to waterfalls, swimming, and a day in the ocean on a kayak. The latter gave me lessons about myself dressed in the mantle of panic: emerging from fear, I decided to live in the solution.

I love to canoe and kayak in streams and gentle rivers. I enjoy the quiet lapping of the water against the boat. The silence of cruising down a stream enables me to see and enjoy the wildlife without disturbing it. I experience calm, and with this peace I have the composure to be able to take nice photos. Even on an estuary such as Moss Landing, with small waves bobbing us, I have found internal stillness. I have enjoyed watching baby and mother sea lions with my grandchildren. There the sea was bouncy but not unruly, so we maintained equanimity in the vessel. The biggest challenge was not to getting too close to the sea animals, as their cuteness and mews were like sirens to me and the kids. We resisted. The whole experience in the streams and in the estuary was serene for me. My desire was to be close to nature, to observe and witness it, not to challenge or overcome it.

For sea kayaking in O'ahu, we also needed life vests and a little training but also a little warning, as this gusty day presented several rows of breakers. We were cautioned on kayak safety and were introduced to a wall-sized map for navigating our course. Our destination was a bird sanctuary island, one of a few islands in a row down the coast and beyond the breakers. We were strongly advised to paddle parallel to the beach beyond the furthermost island and then paddle back at an angle to reach the beach. "Don't try to take a shortcut," our trainer told us. "Go down beyond the islands. Let the tides help you approach the beach at the proper angle, and avoid the underwater shoals. They can be nasty."

They trucked us with our boats to the shore. We unloaded them and started the trek down a path, across a stream and to the beach. Amid much advice-sharing and a little swearing we banged our shins along the way to the shore.

I looked out to those waves, and my blood ran cold. They were huge. The islands were barely visible over the swells and under the sky. Yet I had committed to going, the guys were ready, and the kayaks were on the shore. Our snacks were tucked safely away in the waterproof bag, but not my stomach. It was roiling with distress signals as I contemplated the choppy sea. I was trying to balance my fearful expectations of disaster with the likelihood of an "unlikely event." I was scared! I was not sure I was ready for this.

I looked around. Regular-looking people were getting into their boats, and tour groups of people of all physical aptitudes were heading out to the bird island. They did not look terrified at all. (Yet I have learned over the years not to "judge my insides by other people's outsides," so their guts may have been churning as powerfully as mine—or the sea—for all I knew.)

I did a little self-talk. I was ready, took a deep breath, and got into my kayak. I promptly flipped, was dunked, and got bruised along the right side of my body in several places. I stood up, my heart pounding, my brain screaming at me to just let them go alone. I took another deep breath and got in again. I was nearly hysterical. Then I remembered to breathe deeply (Yoga 101). My husband, after a lot of twists and turns, got in while chasing the boat through the wake, and we were off. We paddled into the oncoming waves, and my heart-rate shot through the roof.

I was trying to keep it together as we faced rolling seas, the waves crashing over the bow and over us pretty regularly. Trying to be helpful, I kept reminding the guys that the kayak trainer had advised us to go out far—but not too far—and ultimately to angle parallel to the beach, overshoot our island by quite a bit, and angle back toward it to avoid the undersea reefs and the powerful currents they created. "Don't try to take a shortcut," he had said.

First off, the guys tried for a short cut. I panicked. I moved into my yoga practice: *First, breathe. Then be sure you are rowing effectively, find your balance, engage your core, and use all your muscles, not just the easy-to-get-to ones. Save your shoulders, your back and your hips from harm. Concentrate on integration. Feel your feelings.*

Oops! My feeling is *panic!!!!* No! No! No! Back to breathing. *Breathe in. Exhale slowly. You are safe. You are strong. You can make it.*

The next step for me was to work through the restraints and the observances—the *Yamas* and the *Niyamas*. The first was non-harming: *Quit yelling at your husband. In spite of the fear, you made the choice to join them. He isn't having the same reactions you are. Leave him be.*

What is the truth? Am I really afraid of dying, or is it just fear of inability and weakness? No, I just don't want to be under the kayak, and I don't want saltwater in my nose. I can deal with that. Breathe.

Stealing? *Clear on that one, well maybe my serenity.*

Attachment? Yes, I am attached to bliss and being calm, and I don't like this anxiety masking as excitement. My ego is also attached to being "one of the guys" and "doing what I committed to" regardless of my concerns. That is on me.

Excess? Yes, I am indulging in my excess of fear, and I am closely in danger of blaming others for my choices. The anger is becoming intoxicating. Am I holding on to the anger to energize me? I am acting like a baby. Looking at the observances, how can I find contentment?

I looked around me. Without the lens of fear, I saw beauty. The water was so rough that the waves had waves...and these wavelets over the reef reflected the sun, where gold, blue, aqua, white and brown all together created a beautiful dappled look such as one might find in beautifully crafted dichroic glass beads. The sun was warm, the islands off the shore were...not close enough! The shore we had come from was too far away as well. *Refocus! Back to the sun on the water and the colors of nature.*

Breathe. I looked to my practices of cleanliness. *Am I clear in my relationships with my husband and with our friend? I am still teetering on the edge of blame. That is not where I want to be. Feel it. Self-study will reveal more on this. Consider discipline and transformational change. The discipline I am practicing is inward-looking, breathing and rowing. Contemplate and practice. Don't give up on any of these.*

This self-investigation reveals that I do not trust. I do not trust my guides to have correctly assessed my abilities (I am weak, I will not be able to handle an emergency, I would not know how to get back into my kayak in this kind of water, and so on.) I don't trust them to find the right path between the shoals and avoid the worst of the waves and currents. They are "guys" and often have an attitude about rules. A suggestion made is one to be challenged. Never mind the warnings or the dangers. I fear they think they know what they're doing, but they're in error. Do I have a flaw in my trust of men? This needs further examination, truly. I love my husband. I really like my friends. But this is all too much! My fear is covering my faith.

Surrender? Yes, this is all I can do. I surrender to the internal journey, as well as the external journey. The breath is my chariot, and I ride to peace. One stroke at a time, I keep pace and stay in motion, and follow directions. I will be OK.

It helped that we made it to the island. I breathed and re-set. I walked on the small beach. The waves were so mighty they blocked the path that wrapped completely around the island. So we wandered back and forth on the beach ate snacks, and I took some nice photos of nesting birds.

We got back into the boats after twenty short minutes and headed back to shore. No, the way back was *not* much easier than the way out, but like a trail horse I returned with renewed vigor, heading for the beach as if my life depended on it. We reached shore, relatively unscathed.

I learned from that experience that I am not a person who takes challenges for pleasure. I enjoy the quiet, the silence, the ease of communing with nature. I am not one to try and conquer her. For me the big lesson was this: breath, awareness, feeling my feelings, and using my physical cues to investigate and understand can guide me through rough water and scary shoals—and I have a big ego that will get me into trouble if I let it do so.

November 11: Moving Is Moving—From Place to Place, in Home or Heart

Change of any type is unsettling, but packing up and closing one's living space to furnish and occupy another is particularly unsettling. Putting belongings in boxes, deciding what to keep and what to give away is hard. Going through "stuff" is the emotional re-experiencing of times past, as well as uncertainty about the future:

- *What will I need in the future?*
- *What can I let go of?*
- *What will I regret having let go of?*

- *What have I never used but have felt necessary to pack with me time and time again?*

Part of the process is selecting what is best for *now*. We cannot know what will be best in the future, but we know a lot about this moment if we listen to it. In the process of moving to a new place is like repeating the steps of recovery, we may notice similar challenges:

- *What is the change of "address" or place in life?*
- *What is the new beginning?*
- *Can we clear out old woes, useless memories, destructive ways of thinking, or mementos that no longer serve to support and enhance our lives?*

Whether we are moving in a physical sense or in a spiritual, emotional or developmental sense, the process is essentially the same: review of the past, evaluation of what we take with us, and re-balancing as we go.

This process is outlined in the steps of recovery. We move from *before* our last drink, drug, binge or similar enmeshment to *after* abstinence has started, and we ask:

- *What will we bring with us into our new life?*
- *What will we leave behind?*
- *Which beliefs and behaviors are to come with on the journey?*
- *Which are to be disposed of?*

In early recovery it was pretty simple. The first pass at the steps taking me from *before* to *after* were elementary: don't use, don't drink, don't lie, don't steal, don't rage, etc. Later I found positive behaviors to develop: patience, trust, reliability, service, kindness to others and myself. These grew slowly. They were my new acquisitions, my soon to be prized possessions.

Looking at times past and revisiting fourth-step material, in addition to keeping the inventory of the tenth step current, has caused me to revisit certain "keepsakes" along the way. I have memories that had previously been neutral: stuff packed away in a vaguely labeled container I had moved from place to place. On further investigation (opening the lid), I found that the contents were *not* as described, "I'm OK." Some were, indeed, troubling and had to be cast off. I needed to re-evaluate generosity when it was based in ego—a desire for recognition. I needed to reconsider justified actions when discovering the resentment that ran beneath it was really the issue. I needed to examine that and let it go. Decisions that had been based on low self-esteem and feelings of unworthiness were no longer valid for me. Hiding behind "I'm OK" were quite a few relics that were now destined for the rubbish heap. This signified that I was moving to a new level, a new tier in my recovery.

This moving, cleaning and sorting is not a one-time process, but a template for living. Practicing it first on recovery, I can apply it to change of jobs or careers, change of physical location, as well as change in any role or relationship. Growth in any form will require *moving*—from one point or perspective to another. Practicing yoga along with the steps can add grace to this process of change. For me, practicing this process has been imperative. Holding on to old ideas is not useful—it is like packing two opposing thoughts into your brain and heart. It is like packing battling creatures in a container. This can be dangerous and a little noisy.

Move gently with yourself, with compassion, as you change any type of landscape in your life.

⚜

May 12: One Day at a Time

"One Day At a Time" used to be the way I got through the week, hand over hand, from one drunken stupor to hangover to the next. I would cry in the shower, twisting the true intention of the phrase to fit my need for inebriation, "Just let me get away with using for one more day." That Christy Lane song would run through my head, singing it for permission to use while knowing I was contorting it from the aim of the lyrics. Little did I know that this song would eventually become my mantra for healing.

While it is said that one should sober up and get clean for oneself rather than another, I got clean thinking of my kids. This, combined with the fear of loss of my soul self, put me over the edge—I was "staring into the abyss" you hear about in the rooms of recovery. I was staring into the void that would be my life. It was shattering. My "loss of self" was wound up in being a mother, which was knotted with knowing what I was doing to my kids. The lack of reliability, stability and care was harming my children. These failings were also failing myself. One day at a time I was making a wreck of our lives. I couldn't go on.

Having had a "phantom mom" is part of my heritage, and it was painful to live through. It took years for me to understand that having an alcoholic mom had an effect on me. And it took many more years to come to terms with it. This emotional abandonment had formed so much of who I was, was to become, and was to overcome. I wanted to spare my kids this challenge. One day at a time, I wanted to be a mom to them, and to reconnect to my own soul-being.

Fast-forward many years. I repaired my relationship with my family. I have spent my years in recovery healing myself and growing whole. I am present. I get up, suit up and show up. And yet I still have bruised parts that are tender to the touch. I listened to a poem video blog last week that chilled me to the bone: "The Countdown of Pain" by Patrick Roche, describing a young person growing up in an alcoholic home. Starting from the present time with his dad's death from an alcohol related accident, he counts backwards through the development of living with an active alcoholic. He ends at birth, when there is such a beacon of hope in the face and life of a newborn. Having recounted his life backwards yhrough the painful adaptation a child makes to live with active addiction, losing the wonder and awe in the superhero parent, and now just trying to stay out of his way. My life was not the same as that of this young man. This poem, however, reminded me of why I became sober and what I feared could happen if I didn't—I certainly didn't want this life to become the life of my children. That was a huge part of the reason I became sober.

I found recovery in two steps: I stopped drinking, and then I stopped drugs. It was hard, I was not immediately better. I had to seek outside help. I also had to convert my street-survival skills to recovery-survival skills. I was sick, I was confused, and I had physical and neurological problems as a result of my drinking and drug abuse. With time I healed. And my kids healed.

One Day at a Time took on new meaning. Rather than living in the future or the past, I had to get through today's issue and challenges with today's tools and resources and today's rewards. They did not always match up: the day was too challenging for my skills, the rewards didn't match the effort, or the challenge was too large for the effort I was willing to make. And then I started to get better: better in my body, mind and spirit; better at deferring gratification; better at knowing what a reward *was*. The reward has been practicing the skills to meet life on life's terms, to enjoy the discipline of being present.

So now, *One Day at a Time* feels just right. It is still a challenge, for when I do things for the first time or do things that feel uncomfortable, I must re-invigorate my learning of the message. I can become emotionally weary or fatigued, but I have resources and tools to refresh myself.

And sometimes I just have to have another "go to sleep" and wake up to the *new* today, to face the new *One Day at a Time*.

❧

May 20: Relapse Triggers and Yoga

Relapse can unfortunately be part of the path to long-term recovery. Along with the steps, counseling, and working with others, yoga is one of the many tools we can use to avoid this unwelcome visitor to our disease.

Catching the relapse [back]slide when it begins can start with an awareness of our emotions. Realization about how we are feeling can prevent full-blown re-engagement with our addictive process. When we find a way to become alert to the sensations in the body, the responses in the gut and muscles that presage backsliding is one of the skills that yoga teaches us.

Life events can leave traumatic footprints. Accidents, divorce, change in economic conditions, frequent relocations, and chronic illness are a few of the events that can leave marks on the psyche and the physiology. Incidents do not have to be overwhelmingly negative to result in being traumatic: they merely need to overwhelm our abilities to adapt at the time, to cope, to rebound.

Those of us who have lived around active addiction have most likely experienced trauma. As anyone whose life has been ruled by uncertainty, inconsistency, and perhaps intermittent rage, anger interspersed with kindness can tell you that these conditions eventually exceed one's ability to readjust and rebalance ourselves. For those of us who have fallen into the well of addiction, trauma is a certainty.

The psychological effects of trauma are an accepted diagnosis and therapy protocols have been developed to address them. What is also known is that the shadows of these events are lodged in the body, in the physical tissues and the physical brain. "The issues live in our tissues" is now a fairly common quotation and phrase. Yoga of 12 Step Recovery, S.O.A.R.(™), TRE(c), and Neurogenic Yoga incorporate an understanding of this awareness. They include movements that include trauma release in their classes and techniques.

Individual talk and group therapies address what is stuck in the mind and emotions. Yoga goes a little further. We are now realizing that we heal better and more thoroughly if we incorporate practices that release emotions trapped in the body. With healing breath practices, *asana* and meditation we combine tools to teach us to feel feelings and offer a way to let them go. Together, yoga therapy, along with other modalities of treatment and support, can affect a total integrated program for healing.

Life In Bite-Sized Morsels

Due to the power of a mindful, therapeutic yoga practice and the power of the breath, care must be taken in their practice. Yoga instructors can gain techniques and greater ability by becoming more aware of the process and effects of trauma. Skilled, compassionate understanding of the sensitivities students touched by trauma may have—sound, the impact of touch, the impact of the language we use when teaching, lighting, arrangement of the students in the room, and many other nuances—can help one maintain a secure space and thereby assist the students in feeling safe and being safe on the mat. In feeling safe, one can let go.

After several years in active recovery and therapy, I found this new location in which *my* past was lodged: my body. I was walking around tightly wound, alternately feeling anxious and afraid or numb and disconnected. I found yoga. Through my yoga practice my body did the talking: yoga gave my body the voice it needed.

Finding the body's voice—the way it can communicate—is only one of the ways relapse is prevented. Another is the release of tension and trauma. The past that had been caught in the body was now being relieved, and the body was reintegrating itself. I was grateful for the release and become more integrated in body, mind and spirit. My recovery path was strengthened, and I was amazed. Looking back, I became well aware that the timeless impact of trauma had put me in danger of relapse. Re-energized to life and thrilled about the change, I conducted research and discovered what I have now come to understand: I had retained my past in my physical body. Yoga practiced in a safe environment, mindfully and slowly, allowed me to release and process these shadows of my past. I found out that I was not alone. Wanting to share this with others, I studied more and learned how to incorporate specific sensitivities into my yoga teaching.

Combining counseling or therapy and sessions with a yoga therapist skilled in yoga for trauma and/or addiction recovery is powerful. If you take yoga classes and have experienced emotional openings on the mat, you may want to pursue additional work privately with a qualified yoga therapist and/or a psychologist to complete the healing cycle: mind, body and spirit. Letting both yoga and other treatment modalities become an integrated part of the rainbow of care reaffirms my recovery and gives me resources to maintain it.

⌘

September 28: Transformation and Music; Musical Transformation

"Transformation is my favorite game, and in my experience, anger and frustration are the result of you not being authentic somewhere in your life or with someone in your life. Being fake about anything creates a block inside of you. Life can't work for you if you don't show up as you."

— Jason Mraz

"Living in the Moment" by Jason Mraz is one of my favorite wake-up tunes. Those few stanzas are packed with wisdom. There are also many recovery songs that reset my system and put me back on the right mental path. Music has the ability to guide my mood to change, to recalibrate my energies into the more upbeat and positive.

I think this young man has a lot of wisdom. It is true: where your authentic self is stifled, so too are the rest of your actions, activities and attitudes. Transformation from the unreal to the real unblocks your energies and allows the genuine self to bloom.

Now, while I am not sure if transformation is a "game," I do know of moves to make to guide myself toward the goal of veracity. The emotional and somatic responses to being false, not true to myself, result in behaviors coming out negative, sideways, in possibly uncontrollable manners. I have strategies at my disposal for feeling safe enough to be real, dealing with fears and anxieties, and finding comfort in being my true self. I have experienced "anger and frustration as the result" of being inauthentic: I can't breathe, my shoulders tighten, my fingers stiffen, my movements become jerky, and my energy gets blocked and trapped around the story I am creating—the one that covers up the real me. I feel bad, so I act badly.

When I take time to acknowledge my physical response to a situation, slow down, and take the time to take stock (a mini-tenth step of body, mind and spirit), I can become aware of and accept my real feelings. Given time, I can trace the source of the discomfort. Often anxiety is based on my concerns about what others think, or what I *think* they think. They are emotions rooted in concerns about being accepted, liked, understood. When left unchecked, these feelings worm in and develop stories. So I "stop, look and listen." I check in, take a moment, take a breath, and look again for the truth—the truth of my authentic being.

I then have a choice. I can choose to stay stuck, or I can be brave. I can be brave and be willing to transform, to take the risk to *be* who I am in spite of the fears I have. That is where the rub of transformation comes in. I am comfortable with discomfort. I have years of experience wearing a mask, covering my true feelings. Anger has been a long-time companion. There is safety in being frozen in anxiety: it means I don't have to try anything new. There can be a sense of grief as I release the old self and embark on the journey to the new. But by initiating a plan to face feelings and change, to remove the mask and face *life on life's terms* authentically, I am making a great leap forward.

To jump back into the "game" of being real I go back to basics; acknowledge feelings, take stock, refresh my view of the goal, take steps. I can be brave in the face of vulnerability once I have found ways to keep myself safe. Finding a landing place in security is critical. This requires that I be in a mental state of calm and have my resources near by-friends, family or trusted mentor. I can be brave when I stay in gratitude and cease dwelling on potential loss (loss of old self, old ways of being or of material concerns). When I let go of the fear of loss I am ready for change;

change that will transform me. And that will let me breathe, loosen up, become more fluid in my body and in my authentic life.

⤳

June 28: My Recovery Is Like a Shark

I was talking to a woman the other day about being active in our recovery program: reading, working the steps, going to meetings, meeting with others, finding ways to be of service in the program, etc. We were sharing the things we do to keep our practice of the program alive. Unexpectedly, the following phrase jumped out of my mouth: "My recovery is like a shark—it will die if I don't keep moving."

Wow—ain't that the truth! No, it isn't just motion for the sake of motion: anger is pretty lively, but that won't keep me emotionally "sober." Though I may feel impatience or frustration, these attitudes will not keep me in healthy waters. Being overly busy and missing the moment by rushing from one thing to another might be active, but it is not recovery.

My recovery-oriented actions include being with others who are healthy and swimming in a wise "school." I like to keep away from the shoals of discontent, self-abasement and frustration, preferring the open seas of unlimited possibilities, hope with my spiritual sky above me.

There are scary deep-sea creatures in the ocean—the gloomy monsters of depression and isolation, those sneaky eels of despair and doubt squirming up to you when you least expect them. There are also those happily dressed-up clownfish, those easy breezy feelings that lure you away from your pack: cockiness, dishonesty or complacency—flighty fish with the temporary treats of activity without consideration of the consequences. These can come in any form of distraction (screen time, for example), another compulsion (such as shopping or eating), or finding another "HP" (him or her)—something or someone that takes me away from my recovery. Swim away, swim away recovery shark! Move toward the light—the spiritual, the good in yourself. Swim to the safe harbor of your recovery friends.

Yes, my recovery is like a shark: I have to keep moving in a wise way. I practice my yoga and stay close to positive people. I read and reflect, meditate and pray. I continue to grow, to learn more, and to stay close to those women I sponsor. Swimming together, they bring out the best in me.

◦⟶∞⟶◦

July 7: Five Ways to Prevent Relapse

I love my fellowship as a group, and I love each person individually. When one member is going through difficulty, we are all affected, and we all feel compassion. When the disease takes one person out, we all mourn. This is a "cunning, baffling and powerful" disease, and we must each remain vigilant to avoid being drawn back into its grasp. This is a patient disease and will wait for us, for any moment of weakness, to beckon to us once again.

The other day I met a man who wants recovery but avoids traditional 12-Step meetings, for he feels confident he can handle recovery on his own. He felt sanguine, but I felt concern. Life is not always rosy—the blush of the newfound sobriety will fade, and one's resolve may not be sufficient; it may pale in face of challenge. The initial critical situation or nudge from judge, spouse or parent may not be sufficient when the pink cloud fades or disappointments mount. At this point, relapsing may be the only way out of a temporary pain.

Being in a habit of hanging out with recovery friends, communicating with sober connections, and having a process to meet obstacles is crucial. Have that habit in place when life turns dark or gray. Some wise advice is available to prevent relapse, much of which has to do with the power of the group:

1. Stay close to your peeps! The "L" of HALT is a warning sign: when isolation looks preferable to community, when alienation feels more comfortable than inclusion, beware! This is a dangerous time, one in which you may be tempted to backslide: to use, to drink, to call "him" or "her," to light a cigarette, to overeat, to call your bookie, or to engage in any of the behaviors we strain to overcome. Instead, get to a 12-Step meeting and be with your *sangha*, your group. Just sit with them in community, quietly. No need to be the center of activity; just *be*—in safety.

2. Be in service. That's right—give away what you may not believe you have. You do have experience, strength and hope, even if it was the experience, strength and hope of yesterday, or even this morning. Sometimes being in need is being of service. Allowing another person to lift you up gives them strength. We share in this seesaw mutual dance of giving and receiving support. But you have to show up, be there, to participate in the dance.

3. Listen to/for the solution. We are not all crazy (or blue) on the same day. Coming to 12-Step meetings and connecting with others will affirm the good and remind you of the not-so-swell. We "tell on" ourselves in meetings; we share our difficulties and our strengths. In compassion and understanding you can see yourself—the good and the struggling. Go to a meeting and hear someone else tell your story. Listen with your whole heart.

4. Pick up the phone. I know this can be archaic, for it's not a text, a tweet, an e-mail or a social posting. *Call.* Why? You have no idea what is going to come out of your mouth! The truth pops out, and you had no idea you "felt like that." The typing and the possible social posturing may in fact obscure your true feelings, so this person-to-person contact is critical (see #1 above).

5. Finally (and foremost), stay close to your higher power. You no longer have to be an "army of one." You are part of it *all*, humanity, the universe and everything! Check in with your higher power frequently. Be close to your HP, practice your communication when you are feeling fine so that the link is there when things are not so fine. Alone, we are in danger. Reach out. Stay in the tribe, the pack, the *sangha*, the *kula*, the posse. Stay with your peeps and keep the addiction at bay. When they are not available, in the dawn of day or the gloom of night, pray. With your higher power, you are not alone.

Many other relapse prevention tools are available: getting to know yourself, knowing your feelings, taking steps to be in good health, knowing your danger/trigger points, etc. Having these tools handy could save your life.

❧

July 26: Meeting Students Where They Are

There is so much pain in the world. Some pain meets us early in life; some is found as we grow; some happens to us as the result of accidents or at the hands of others; some we bring on ourselves. Add to this an incurable disease such as addiction, and you have a recipe for disaster and the potential for lifelong suffering.

Addiction can include any of a number of destructive behaviors: unhealthy relationships, food, gambling, unwise sex, or substance addiction such as tobacco, drugs and alcohol, some embraced first for *fun* and then continued to the brink of destruction. Addictions can become the focus of our lives. Certain behaviors can also result from having grown up in unhealthy homes and destructive circumstances—the pain the world has put before us without our choice or consent. Growing up in a dysfunctional home results in a variety of destructive behaviors, from total lack of trust in others and self to impulse control issues and low self-esteem. Other coping behaviors can include the need for control, or self-protective behaviors such as anger or rage. The extremes of these can manifest in physical and psychic disturbances. These attitudes and beliefs influence how we think, act and behave. Ultimately, they change how our brains are formed and how they function.

Once we have found a recovery program, how do we stay on the path of health? Many people have found yoga in addition to their other tools and programs. Their practice on the mat and investigation of yoga philosophy has greatly enhanced their healing. We came together to share the power of a recovery yoga practice with one another. We also share the possibility of transformation with each other. We recalibrate our feelings and reactions as we learn to sense them. Yoga helps us to inhabit our bodies and feel feelings as they reveal themselves physically in belly, breath and chest. By experiencing how we feel before we act, we transform previous unhealthy behavior into positive choice.

Yoga is such a powerful practice. The practices and poses restore us to physical and emotional balance. The postures can also release tensions and traumas. While this is magical, the process must be presented in a safe, supportive manner. This is profoundly true when teaching people who are especially vulnerable. Students who are newly clean and sober come to the mat with a variety of abilities and restrictions. "Meeting the students where they are," the yoga teacher's mantra, is crucial.

With people in early recovery, though, *knowing* where *you*, as a teacher, are on that continuum is often a challenge. It is a big part of the teacher's practice to become vividly aware of one's own feelings and attitudes, expectations and prejudices—yes, prejudices. I have pre-judgments on many things. I have pre-formed ideas about all manners of aspects of living, from what it is like to be detoxing to what it is like to practice with an old injury. I also may believe I know what it is like to try yoga when one comes from a background or a cultural heritage unlike my own. It is naive to think that I, as a teacher, might not have a bias, a preconception or an expectation. It is not wrong to have these; it is merely unskilled not to investigate them. With care, I investigate, note and consider my attitudes. This has opened two things: self-empowerment through self-examination, and a greater compassion to understanding how others may feel, particularly when they may be limited by *their* own glasses.

We, as teachers, can be wise, cautious and careful in introducing our students to their abilities. Additionally, how we describe the poses and the postures can be of great use to our students. Bringing recovery language and principles into our teaching can make all the difference—the difference between yoga as an exercise activity and yoga as an integrated part of the recovery program. Teachers who are open, authentic and inquisitive bring a richness into their teaching. They can help turn the coal of the past into gems in the present. Trained teachers in the field of recovery yoga can come to the mat with innate kindness, without attachment, with minimal pre-judgment, and with compassion.

※

August 9: Habits of the Mind and the Seventh Step

I was reading about the seventh step in the book *Twelve Steps and Twelve Traditions* (the 12 x 12) a few weeks ago. It reminded me about the importance of letting my higher power be in charge of removing my defects of character. I constantly think that I must be in charge of exactly when and how my shortcomings should be addressed. In that regard, and in many others, I have suggestions about how my HP should work in my life. I think I am the one who knows when my unhealthy attitudes, actions and behaviors need to be altered and improved. Mostly it is *right now, in this situation, for this reason.*

Further reading and contemplation has changed my understanding. While I am in charge of being ready...my HP is in charge of the rest. This might not be news to others, but it has taken me several "trips around the sun" to really read what is being written in the literature and not just pick words out at random, thereby creating my own internal text and understanding.

In the 12 x 12, we are urged to become ready "without delay." The Seventh Step prayer goes further, stating that we are asking for removal of those defects that "stand in the way of my usefulness to you and my fellows." I might not be aware of what specific defects are currently in my way. I might think that impatience is vexing me and frustrating my need to intersect in an activity in a certain way, but actually tenacity may be the skill needed to allow a situation to unfold. My idea might be to plow through, but the idea of "God's Time, Not Mine" may be in play. I still have to do footwork, but the timing of the result or outcome is not up to me.

By putting one's higher power in charge of the choosing, we are not looking at the defects and making the selection. To me, this means I am also relieved of perseveration—of concentration and focus on my defects. I do not need to focus on planning, scheming and offering them up for removal. I don't need to keep thinking about my list of defects, looking at it, evaluating it for change, measuring them from one day to the next. Instead, I am keeping my eye on being useful, on living a good life, and on focusing my daily intentions on the good and the positive. This creates a healthy habit of the mind. This also develops a positive form of thinking and behavior. Looking at the negative, the thoughts and actions that are not so useful are...not so useful. Reflecting on the unlovely can become a habit that decreases my healthy self-esteem. Looking toward the goodness, the improvement, and the growth is helpful. This can decrease the negative *samskara* (habits of the mind), as we call it in yogic traditions, and can create new, healthful mental grooves and thought patterns.

Just for today, I will encourage my mind to the health and wellness of my thoughts—and leave the degree and substance of the removal of my shortcomings to my HP.

❦

September 11: Yoga and Recovery Month

With the auspicious co-occurrence of Yoga Awareness Month and Recovery Month both in September, it is the perfect time for me to share my five important recovery benefits from practicing yoga:

1. Getting acquainted with feelings. When I was a newcomer, first entering the room of my 12-Step program, I had no idea what my feelings were. I had the basics: sad, mad and glad, but even these were not experienced in appropriate amounts or expressed in proper circumstances. My emotional wiring had shorted out. Fast-forward a few years, and I have developed a rainbow of feelings and have become more skilled at expressing them, in the right volume and in the proper circumstance.

Then came the period in my "teens" of recovery in which I lost touch with myself. I had difficulty identifying my own personal feelings; I felt blocked and out of touch. Enter yoga: what an amazing experience... union of body, mind and spirit, one pose, one breath at a time. I had no idea this would happen, yet on the yoga mat I began to get in touch with my feelings. It began with noting physical sensations. Where did I feel effort? Where did I feel ease? With time I began to investigate my responses to the sensations: how did I feel about effort? How did I feel about the challenging poses? How did my heart and my mind deal with that? Did I try extra hard? Did I recoil from the pose? Did I dread trying a difficult posture, or did I feel I was in battle with it, pushing through to conquer it? I realized that how I dealt with my yoga practice was how I dealt with life. It became a window and a mirror. It helped me to learn my feelings and feel the process of learning.

2. Slow Growth with Gratitude. I am not a spring chicken. I am a woman of a certain age, and I am grateful for my time on this planet. As with many in the rooms of recovery, one of the outcomes of my past life could have been death or disability. I am so fortunate to be here, well and healthy. My chronological age does not trouble me. When I am in a yoga class and look around at others, I see youth, flexibility, strength, and all kinds of abilities I do not possess—oops, that is judging myself by their outsides...not so helpful. When I bring myself back to my own mat, and participate in my own practice as I must participate in my own recovery, I am able, from day to day, from practice to practice, to see progress...not weight loss, arm balance mastery, or movement into any pretzel pose, but composure, steadiness, stillness and ease. As in practicing the principles of the program, the change comes, "sometimes swiftly and sometimes slowly." I notice the changes, and I am grateful.

3. Discipline and Commitment. It is not always easy to get to a 12-Step meeting. Nor is it always easy getting to a yoga class. It requires commitment and dedication—to yourself and to your growth. I know I will feel better. I know my mind will move away from planning or per-severation when I practice my yoga. I can't think about the grocery list when I move through my fourth slow sun salutation or balance in half-moon pose for ten slow, full breaths. I just can't balance and be in the poses when my mind wanders. I can balance and be there when I stay in my body, feeling my feelings, witnessing my mind, and being in the moment. That is the grace of the practice. Even when I experience joy while coming out of final relaxation, I occasionally fight attendance to my practice. I procrastinate, I make excuses, I resist—just like going to 12-Step meetings. And yet, nothing can be better than keeping that commitment. It is an estimable act—helping to build self-worth.

4. Integration. One definition of yoga is *union:* union of body, mind and spirit. I am an addict/alcoholic. I have a physical allergy and a spiritual malady, and I suffer from a mental obsession. This makes yoga a perfect remedy—a holistic remedy for this holistic disease. Through the breath and through the poses we calm the mind. In fact, the mind may even soften to the point that thinking retreats into the background and one can get into a meditative state just experiencing the pose, the breath, and one's higher power. In our 12-Step meetings we move toward the 11th and 12th steps, creating in ourselves the capacity to both pray and meditate, as well as to be right in our thoughts, actions and deeds in our daily lives. We do this so we may be of service. And through Karma yoga we also practice being of service by coming from the place of our higher selves. In this way we have developed integration of body, mind and spirit, and we practice this both on and off the mat.

5. Trust. Now, you might wonder, how does yoga affect trust? I first wondered how going to meetings was going to keep me sober! I was also curious as to how working the 12 Steps would improve my life. It was in a shambles...and yet, trusting in the process, I came to meetings, met with another alcoholic, read and worked the steps, and now, many years later, I no longer doubt. I trust. I am not flexible, I am stiff, I don't have one of "those" bodies, and I have a mind that whirls around and seemingly cannot stay still, so how was I going to practice yoga, and how was I going to relax in *savasana* (tranquility pose)? I trusted. I stepped onto the mat, slowly the pain in my wrists evaporated, and I could do downward-facing dog without my awareness of my hands and forearms distracting me from my breath. My forward-fold became less stunted and strained and became more fluid and full of ease. I gave myself time to improve and learn. I trusted my body to know what was OK and what was safe, and I worked within that capacity. I don't do elaborate back bends—they are not for me. It took a few experiences with pain to confirm this, but now I know. I have trusted both my limits and my abilities. I have taken this knowledge into my experiences off the mat and realize I do some things with ease and other things with difficulty, and some things I have a choice about. Self-trust is huge, and it is a very worthy benefit from both the recovery and the yoga practice.

These five things are but a scratch on the surface of mutual benefits. Sharing from the heart, reading recovery material, and practicing a healthy lifestyle including yoga can enrich and enliven your life, enhancing your present and preventing relapse in your future.

❦

March 23: Yoga and Trauma

We who have lived around active addiction have experienced trauma at some level. Anyone whose life has been ruled by uncertainty, inconsistency, intermittent rage, anger interspersed with kindness, etc., has experienced trauma. Those who have had surgeries, been in accidents or endured direct violence have experienced trauma as well.

All of these events are lodged in the body as well as the psyche. Individual talk and group therapies address what is stuck in the mind and emotions. We are now realizing that we heal better and more thoroughly if we also address the feelings that are trapped in the body. Yoga and simple breath practices can release these traumas trapped in our bodies. Together, yoga therapy, combined with other modalities of treatment and support, can affect a total integrated program for healing.

As a woman in recovery and a "victim" of childhood and adulthood chronic and "shock" traumas, I became well aware of the timeless impact of these events when I became in danger of relapse. I discovered what I have now come to understand as the retention of negative past experiences in my physical body. Yoga, practiced in a safe environment, mindfully and slowly, allowed me to release and process these shadows of my past.

If you are in therapy, consider working with a yoga therapist skilled in yoga for trauma and/or addiction recovery. If you take yoga classes and have experienced emotional openings on the mat, you may want to pursue additional work privately with a qualified yoga therapist and/or psychologist to complete the healing cycle: mind, body and spirit. S.O.A.R.(™)-certified yoga teachers, among others, can bring this awareness to the mat in all venues: studios, treatment centers and other spaces.

Some yoga classes seem more designed for the physical practice: power yoga, hot yoga, yoga that is physically demanding. These classes can help break through some barriers or bring a level of challenge and exhaustion that is effective for some. This fast, active practice can also trigger and/or continue some unhealthy "overdoing" patterns, which can be counterproductive.

A slow, deliberate, thoughtful yoga practice can be as physically challenging and can become meditative: giving the student time to experience the sensations of the poses rather than exclusively the feeling of effort. Slow yoga also helps to calm the mind and reduce the hamster-wheel running of the thoughts, not just in the class; there are lingering effects after class.

Include yoga along with other treatment modalities: therapy, 12-Step meetings, and work with other health practitioners. Let yoga become an integrated part of your rainbow of care.

RESOURCES AND REVIEWS:
Recovery, Rather than the Pain of Active Addiction, Gratefully Makes its Way Into the Culture

I AM FORTUNATE to live in an area that is filled with creative, dedicated people. I know people who have performed in plays about the early days of AA. I have been to screenings of movies and enjoyed music that celebrates the fun and challenges of being in recovery. I have been able to enjoy a wide variety of healing- and recovery-oriented plays, movies, books and music. Every time I hear a musician include recovery words in her lyrics, I am heartened. When an author or artist breaks anonymity, I feel part of a healing circle. I have attended plays written by a talented young woman in the San Francisco Bay area: Jackie B. She has written *In Our Own Words* (Bill and Bob's story) and *Our Experience Taught Us* (a story of the 12 Steps coming together.) I have seen the Greg Williams movie *The Anonymous People*. This powerful documentary about the history and purpose of AA and the importance of openly celebrated recovery is affecting the way society is viewing addiction and addiction treatment. I enjoy the music of Sonia Lee and other artists who are bringing the language and principles of recovery into musical genres of all types, including all ages, in the celebrations of a clean, sober life.

I also include in my resources books by people who are in recovery, for whom recovery is an integral part of life's challenges. Lawrence Block and J.A. Jance include recovery themes in their mysteries, and the world of literature is lifted and enhanced by all the writings of Anne Lamott. They have all influenced me, expanded my enjoyment of recovery, and contributed to my understanding of the struggle to get here.

The world wasn't ready for John Larroquette's 1990s comedy series *The John Larroquette Show*, about a bus station night manager in recovery. This sleeper of a series took the viewer through the 12 Steps in the first twelve episodes. I was enthralled and uplifted by this public acknowledgement of recovery, but it didn't appeal to the public and faded after a few seasons. Much more to the public's liking were characters with active addiction issues who were apparently able to hold down responsible jobs in *House*, *Breaking Bad*, *Nurse Jackie*, etc., as well as characters who weave sobriety into their roles: Sherlock on *Elementary*, Detective Andrew Flynn on *Major Crimes*, and Leo McGarry of *West Wing*. These examples of the pain of use followed by the practice of recovery have positively reinforced my clean, sober living.

Comedy has its proponents, too—comedians who have stepped out of the shadow of anonymity to create works about the sober life. Mark Lundholm and Kurtis Matthews have spearheaded Recovery Comedy tours and routines for recovery conferences and other events.

Recovery music has grown from the online-streaming 12StepRadio. com to conventions and informal gatherings. Independent publishing has allowed the recording and distribution of a wide variety of recovery-oriented music. The lyrics and beats range from traditional rock-and-roll to ballads to hip-hop and other current styles, all with a recovery theme.

I have sometimes written about my experience with these media. Not all are reviews in the formal sense, though some are. They are primarily musings about the effect these tendrils have on my life, reassurance that I am on the right path, and that people and characters I admire share this path.

❧

January 3: *Imperfect Birds* by Anne Lamott

While cuddling up with a book is not a classical yoga position, taking time for self-care, self-study, contentment and contemplation are all yogic practices. So "cuddle up" was the pose I assumed for an hour each day last week as I read Anne Lamott's book *Imperfect Birds*. Lamott takes the reader through the challenges of sobriety, balance, being a parent, and being one's self. This book chronicles a few months in the lives of a North Bay (San Francisco Bay) family, telling the story of the deep dive into madness and disarray addiction takes the individual, the family and their friends, and its effect on the community. For those of us who were "the teenager" going from "experimentation" as a form of escape (or entertainment) to addiction, and for those of us who are or were parents of "future fellows" (of the rooms of NA or AA), this book lends its bald, honest, authentic voice to that journey. No one comes out unscathed or unchanged. The annealing process of finding yourself and finding sobriety is forged of pain, letting go, and waking up. Lamott guides the reader through the twists and turns, hopes and denials, false starts and restarts that occur along the way.

Lamott adds enough sweet humor and tender insights into one's humanness to make that process bearable. In the end you find yourself in each one of her characters—the addict, the co-addict, the healer, the helper. This book brought me back to the basics of my AA recovery program, my recovery from being a child of an alcoholic, and my recovery as an Al-Anon—the disease of over-helping. It also brought me to the basics of self-care—that sometimes a dose of couch-cuddling with a fabulous book is just what the body ordered. Thank you, Anne.

⊰⊱

June 30: *Bill W. and Dr. Bob* and Women in Recovery

I had a great time last week at the play *Bill W. and Dr. Bob* by Stephen Bergman and Janet Surrey at the San Jose Rep with friends. We started the evening with a delicious, fragrant meal at a Thai restaurant. Taking our time, chatting up a storm, eating and visiting with one another, we were in danger of missing the opening curtain. Fumble-rushing out of the restaurant and across the street to the theater, we made it to our seats in time to admire the fabulous stage setting and get settled for the play.

The incredible actors brought this poignant play to life as they told the story of the founding of AA. The play begins in the depth of despair of active alcoholism and ends with the forming of the first group of recovery. This was not a linear, planned path. It was replete with failures and backsliding, in terms of personal sobriety and concepts for a stable group.

The torment and role of the wives was depicted realistically as well—the desire to help and guide as well as the experience of the personal losses and shame that accompany any family living through the hell of active addiction. The indefatigable grip on hope these women had was both confusing and inspirational. The play's era explained a lot; life for women in the '30s and '40s was different that it is today. Yet today, that same degree of devotion, despite the social and economic consequences, is still in evidence. All manners of addiction and all genders of spouse are subject to the grips of co-addiction and co-dependence. This play gave a taste of what that could be like.

It also reminded me that alcoholics are as different as they are similar: not all men drink alike, nor get sober alike. Bill was a carouser, and Dr. Bob was a solitary drinker. Yet they both ended up the same way—full of confusion, pain and hopelessness—and came to find healing in recovery the same way—through spiritual experience, mutual support and helping others. They expanded and solidified these experiences with the development of the guidelines of service, along with the early versions of the Steps.

I was struck once again by how different the path to recovery can be for many women. For the most part we don't have the "support" system in the form of a spouse that provides us with prepared meals, clean clothes, and the constant urging that we "are better than that." Most often wives and women do the behind-the-scenes work of food, shopping, cooking, etc., in addition to drinking themselves into oblivion.

And yes, those chores become more and more perfunctory as time and disease go on.

House cleaning and meal preparation are only some of the ways the woman's experience can differ from the man's. The shame that comes from promiscuous behavior is different for men than it is for women. The burden of childcare still rests mainly on the moms, so child neglect and other traumas may weigh particularly hard on women's shoulders. Not that men don't feel remorse or guilt in this area, but women have more of a landscape of responsibility, hence a greater area of guilt and shame. Females have other challenges as well. We women in the program are used to "translating" the Big Book to be more gender-neutral (and still struggle with the chapter, "To the Wives"). We are grateful for the expanded examples in the back of the book's fourth edition, but the book's concepts and suggestions are not applicable to all people, particularly not to most women.

These issues are not the subject of *Bill W. and Dr. Bob*, but that play did get me to think again about the silence of women in recovery. I would love to see a play about women in recovery, e.g., about Marty Mann and the beginning of the recovery movement's strong female voices. For we women possess a special shame and must follow a special course to discover self-love and find healing. Many of us experience challenges in our recovery that are different from men's: the right sizing of our egos, the types of self-forgiveness, and the creation of boundaries and autonomy, to name a few.

⊰❧⊱

May 3: *The Anonymous People* and Secrets

"We are only as sick as our secrets." This is a phrase used in my anonymous program to encourage us to let go (in an appropriate and confidential manner) those things that fester inside, preventing us from feeling free and able to grow and moving on from our past.

Guilt, shame, and lies will erode my recovery and can bring me to the verge of, if not actually into, relapse. Identifying these secrets and sharing them with another can relieve me of the isolation of shame, keep me on the path of recovery, and help me take steps to remediate problems from the past.

Seeing *The Anonymous People* furthered my thinking about the final secret: *anonymity*. When I was working, I didn't (immediately) tell my bosses that I was a woman in long-term recovery. I was also afraid to disclose that on my insurance company applications, and only in the quiet of a nearly empty lunchroom would I share the information with a colleague in confidence. I wouldn't tell anyone about my destination when I would go to a lunchtime recovery meeting. To do so would have brought confusion, anxiety and concern on both our parts—and, I feared, disdain on theirs. The shame of having this disease was kept alive by the concern that my workmates would no longer trust me, that my boss and coworkers would be uncertain about my reliability and might worry about the potential of relapse. All of that kept my guilt and shame a strong undercurrent and contributed to my inability to accept myself completely.

Addiction is not treated as a disease like diabetes, heart disease, or HIV infection. Our tradition of anonymity may account for that. While anonymity is critical in not revealing one another's membership in a program of recovery, lest we are seen as representatives for a particular recovery program, we seem to use this mandate to keep ourselves and our recovery in the dark. When we do so, we also keep our successes in the dark.

We in recovery force our families, the co-addicts, to keep a secret. Yet again, even in recovery, they have to learn to stuff a secret to protect their loved one who suffers from a disease. Is this healthy? The pain around being an adult child of an alcoholic, the spouse of an alcoholic (or other addict), or the parent of an addicted child is enormous. There is a built-in layer of guilt and shame, the unending mental repetitions of "if only," which implies that you could have stopped the process of the illness as if you could think your way out of kidney disease. You can't.

They can't. Does keeping this one last secret underscore the misguided conception of control and avoidance? Are we shielding ourselves, the co-addict, from harm by association? Would revealing the disease cause relapse? How does this shielding contribute to the misinformation about the disease of addiction? Does silence mean that this is not an illness? By protecting the identity of a family member with a disease, are we not contributing to the negative perception of this disease? Finally, are we denying others the joys and rejoicings of recovery?

The Anonymous People made these and other important points about recovery. Not only are we not able to celebrate our recovery and rebirth to health as we stay in the shadows, but the journey and difficulties leading to acute addiction and the support required for full recovery remain a public mystery. HIV/AIDS, diabetes, cancer, heart disease and others are all conditions for which there is treatment but no cure (as of yet, and their prevention and treatment have amazing public support. Events, races, and social media campaigns fund further research and bring public awareness. Hospitals and medical centers have built their reputations on their advances in those fields. In the yoga community I find tremendous support and funding for Yoga for Cancer, Yoga for Heart Health, Yoga for Chronic Pain due to Arthritis and Diabetes, etc., though Yoga for Addiction Recovery & Relapse Prevention and Yoga for Youth, programs designed to avert early onset of addiction, get short shrift in funding and in public attention. This is what silence gets us. We shun ourselves and our recovery, creating an atmosphere of rejection and neglect.

Even with the advent of Recovery Month (September), the growth of the awareness campaigns is still slow. *The Anonymous People* broadens the understanding of the recovery path and opens up the conversation about addiction recovery. Hopefully more and more people can gain an understanding in these 88 minutes of education, revelation and discussion. Hopefully the research on prevention and recovery resources can gain more much needed funding and treatment times, and processes can be appropriately lengthened for this fatal illness.

≈

July 21: Yoga and Early Intervention: Kids Can Self-Care

Breathing, centering, sensing how you feel without resistance and without action—what if I had access to these tools as an adolescent? What would I have considered as viable options to the risks I took, the dangers I sought, and the chemicals I ingested? Would a safe place with support that offered tools to address my anxieties and emotions have prevented or delayed my trajectory into active addiction?

I grew up in a house that offered little security: one parent was alcoholic, and the other lived away from the home, often out of the country. It was a household of economic uncertainty, cyclical extreme poverty, emotional upheavals, and fear. What was I to do with feelings? There were no adults to provide certainty or guidance, and my job as the eldest was to provide those things for my younger siblings. I intuitively knew they needed security, but was powerless to find it for myself.

If the statistics on *when* one starts to use drugs and alcohol are correct, the earlier in life one starts drinking and using, the more likely one will become addicted to substances, long-term brain function will be impaired, emotional and intellectual disability will be more entrenched. I started early, and the damage was intense and deep. It took many years of hard work with the help of others to knit myself back together. I had to find people who could teach me healthy resources and tools. I needed to find ways to know what I was feeling, to discern one emotion from the next in the right size to a proper degree, and to act on them appropriately.

Some of these skills had been learned by others in their youth: breathing, centering, sensing your feelings. What if you had those kinds of options as a kid? What if schools, church groups, and (yes) caregivers like parents could teach you ways to slow down, to feel, to consider, and then to act? A recent article in the *Journal of Adolescent Health*, "Yoga-Based

Breathing Techniques Can Help Reduce Teen Impulsive Behavior: Study," argues that early interventions with such techniques can help reduce impulsive behavior in teens (Partnership for Drug-Free Kids, July 15, 2013, Drugfree.org). This study, conducted in Los Angeles, followed a group of teenagers, some who participated in the YES! (Youth Empowerment Seminar!) and some who did not. The statistically significant positive results indicated that the students who participated reported less impulsive behavior than before.

The Niroga Institute in Oakland has brought yoga techniques into schools for years. B.K. Bose founded the Institute to offer classes for all people from all backgrounds and walks of life. Niroga offers training to certify yoga teachers in this specialty. Niroga has teachers ready to go—the schools and facilities have only to ask. Could we fund prevention, rather than incarceration and treatment?

Through Niroga I taught at the San Jose Job Corps. It was an amazing experience: between 12 and to 25 kids would meet twice a week in the gym, where we would breathe, move, and create a sacred space they all "defended" with their admonition to "respect the teacher," "take off your shoes and leave your worries on the side," and "Hey, check this out—breathe like this, man! You won't be so pissed!" Their peaceful faces in the final pose, *savasana*, reminded us all of the goodness we *all* want to have and be. Do these kids now have one more tool in their quiver? I trust so.

Whether it is Niroga, Y.E.S. or Street Yoga, we are all there in the heart of prevention, empowerment, and support of our youth. As usual, funding is lacking. This is a crime against youth—the most vulnerable among us with the most to offer.

Let's bring effective programs such as these into our schools. We can train teachers, we can train aides, we can teach the kids. For as little as 100 breaths a day, we can give our kids choices.

❧

January 19: Kids Can Have a Voice, Too

Many years ago I had wanted to write a book about my addiction and the pain it was inflicting on my kids. Not yet ready to renounce my addiction, I was reaching back into my own childhood for my experiences and combining them with what I was doing in my own home to my two toddlers. The booklet was titled "My Mommy Drinks Too Much," and I typed this sentimental work while inebriated, complete with strikeouts, on onion-skin paper, as I imagined all true authors did. To really get to their feelings, they had to drink. And so did I. That was what I thought made good writing.

So off it went, my poorly typed manuscript with incomplete thoughts and ideas, filled with pain and remorse, self-loathing and shame. I pitied the poor women at New Seed Press who received it! But they were as kind as they could be when they got back to me, suggesting further development and rewrites. I put the piece away and didn't consider writing for another thirty years.

Writing for children is an amazing skill—to bring life to weighty topics in a way that is accessible to kids, neither talking down to them nor talking over their heads. What I had tried to do in the 1980s, Jody Lamb has successfully and beautifully done in 2012. *Easter Ann Peter's Operation Cool* (Scribe Publishing) is a touching story of 12-year old Easter Ann, who is trying to establish her own identity in her school while dealing with her mom, an active alcoholic "too sick" to participate in so much of Easter Ann's life. Dad is oblivious to this and Easter Ann continually tamps down her own needs for attention and affection with excuses as her mom's drinking continues.

As we meet Easter Ann, she is entering seventh grade, a tender, vulnerable age. In spite of conditions in her home, she is eternally upbeat, getting out of bed each morning with bright hope like a spring sparrow, with wishes for the day to be positive and different. She heads off to school to make a difference in her life, embarking on "Operation Cool," a way to connect and find new friends. How she can possibly do this with the weight of her own upbringing and caretaking on her shoulders is beyond anyone's ability. Understating and denying her fears and dread about her mom's condition, she valiantly takes over the duties of the parent from breakfast through dinner, to make everything seem "all right." But the hope that blossomed in her heart on arising is dashed each afternoon when she returns home as the mom she desperately misses glides through the house from bed to porch and back again without so much as an acknowledgment that her dear daughter has now been abandoned.

Three months after we meet Easter Ann, the family finally wakes up to her mom's alcoholism. In this story, for this girl, there *is* a family—a grandmother, an aunt, and a father who eventually opens his eyes to what he had been ignoring: this woman, his wife, needs help. The family seeks guidance and confronts the mom, offering sufficient support for things to change. In addition, Easter Ann finds a community of healing—and that is one cool operation.

I loved the book. I have read it several times. It makes me cry. I cry for myself, who was in Easter Ann's place for many more years, with a sister and a brother to care for. I didn't have the support of my extended family, nor did we have an intervention to guide us through the rocky shoals of relapse and recovery. We didn't have a supportive father who believed in us and what we were going though. My tears at reading this book are those of understanding, compassion, sorrow, and a little envy. I identify with Easter Ann's can-do attitude. I understand her love of animals, that giving of care and kindness that you yourself seek. I identify with her ability to regard school as a haven, albeit sometimes not so safe, but a place with a certain sense of order and predictability. Whenever I read *Easter Ann Peter's Operation Cool,* I cry for all of those who have neither school nor pets nor healthy friends nor family to support them as they navigate the waters of this unholy disease.

COMMUNITY AND CONFERENCES
Our Community Both Challenges and Sustains Us

———— ❧ ————

BEING PART OF a community has been key to my recovery. In fact, community is now a far-reaching concept: I have developed many pods of peeps. When I was using and drinking, my only "friends" were those who used or drank as I did, and those who could put up with me. In early recovery I had only my recovery friends, but they were close to where I was emotionally: not yet mature, often still embroiled in codependent and immature relationships. It was all I could handle at the time. I yearned to have the confidence and stability of those women with long-term sobriety. I wanted to dress and act like a person with class. I wanted to be respected and act respectfully. That took a while, as I had always been attracted to the wild ones, the scruffy ones, the bad boys and the girls who loved them.

Now I am a little more dignified and graceful, and I have additional circles of friends. I am connected to people who practice yoga, do ceramics, write, sing, and perform. I have circles within circles in my family, including the ex-spouses and "step" kids. I have also been able to watch my kids grow and their circles expand. With greater feelings of stability and confidence, they have more productive lives in school, professions, hobbies, families and friends. I participate either directly with or through them as they share their amazing journeys with me and we have a healthy give-and-take about our lives and our experiences.

I am also involved in online communities that focus on healing, recovery, yoga, and yoga service. These groups expand my *sangha* beyond my geographical area, and even beyond my native tongue. I have active conversations, with people in South America, India, Spain and beyond. I am a participant in and contributor to online recovery forums and meetings. I share writing and resources with yoga students and teachers across North America. These relationships enhance my understanding of what it means to be a participant in and citizen of the world, thus enriching my sense of goodness in the divine universe.

Conferences develop community by bringing like-minded people together for sharing and education and enlarging the circle of commonality. Conferences are also partial retreats offering ways to renovate and restore oneself. Professional and personal connections can be made; and often these can last a lifetime. Conferences can also open one up to new ideas, new ways to look at things, new possibilities that stretch current paradigms. Not all are comfortable or easy—but they do expand community, even when provocative and challenging.

Finding and connecting with community in all forms—formal and familial, friendly and formidable—is now possible for me, now that I am in recovery. My world has broadened, and my life is full.

⌗

January 11: Esalen at the Yoga, Meditation and Addiction Recovery Conference

I went to Esalen for the second annual meeting of the Yoga and Addiction Recovery Conference (YARC) in late October, which was held during the monarch butterfly migration for the second time. Was that an accident, or a wonderful coincidence? Last year it was so cold the poor insects were grounded on the paths and in the dirt, caught in mid-transformation, in need of care. Artful signs were placed here and there to alert us to their plight and caution us to tread carefully with mindful foot placement, so we stepped with care to avoid them.

As this conference is a place for introspection to effect change, I, too, could be caught cold in mid-transformation, needing care. I felt that way my first year at the YARC. I was unsure about my decision to attend, about having come, noting my feelings about participation: being part of, but mostly apart from, the event, "grounded" in self-doubt, laying low, waiting for the temperature to rise so I could continue my recovery journey

This second year at YARC had warm air for the butterflies and a more evolved internal landscape for me, so we were both more mobile. Like the monarchs, who now flitted from bush to bush, I moved from new-found friendship group to friendship group. With more confidence and comfort in the large group I was more "active in my own recovery," embracing the new with tenderness and vulnerability but also with balance and greater core security.

Through the YARC I was changing my life direction, connecting with large numbers of people I didn't know. I was challenging my previous discomfort with large groups—occasionally feeling internally out of balance and externally feeling isolated even in a group of people. I was in part integrating within myself and in part finding myself as I offered a supportive role to newcomers and young women in recovery. This is a conventional source of contradiction between needs and skills, one that stems back to my youth, when I often needed help but found myself providing it.

A year later, raw in yet another way and still overwhelmed with seventy plus yogis in recovery, I accept this feeling of vulnerability. I remind myself time and time again that there are no "shoulds" in terms of recovery, comfort or change. I can only harm myself by thinking I "should" be comfortable with all people at all times and "should not" feel anxious in a new situation or discomforted with new revelations about myself and my journey. "Shoulds" are not useful. Learning to adapt to a new situation may require new tools, and it happened to take me a year to gain facility with them.

This third year was a time to be able to be where I was, to openly relate to what was being taught in the workshops, in the dining hall, and through walking with friends and talking at night in the cabin; sitting in the tubs, or standing at the fence gazing at the ocean. The teachings were available everywhere, and I was ready to absorb, investigate and integrate them.

So, like the sun-soaked monarchs, I flitted from cluster to cluster of generous yogis who shared themselves, their metamorphoses, with me in the warm, sometimes windy sunshine of the week. And while this year's YARC was a far more comfortable experience than last year's, things still shifted inside of me; I still felt some discomfort and disunion. Which made it clear that I still had some healing to do, which was good. I was able to retain feelings of security, serenity, and the sensation of being sacred just as I am. Could I have found those feelings without having begun with vulnerability and pain? I am not sure. I opened, became vulnerable, and in flooded pain, from both inside and outside—more precisely, from my *interpretation* of the outside.

There were times when my mind tended to judge rather than witness, criticize rather than observe and note. What was said by others was not always heard by me. Instead, I heard my own misinterpretations or illusions of what was said. So I felt pain, separation from others, and many of the other negative sensations experienced by a tender mind in recalibration and recovery.

To heal from the feelings of separation and separateness back into the land of "us" and community, I needed to go back to my tool kit. I practiced all of the means at my disposal for self-care. I wrote, meditated, and took time for myself away from activity, busyness, and distractions of games, hot tubs and conversation. I read and I rested. I found security in my ability to care for myself, and I found grace. Wellness starts inside with "an attitude of gratitude." When I was ready to re-enter the community, I experienced the good fortune of having people around me who cared a great deal for me and were content just to be there as comfort and witness as I worked things through. It didn't really matter if the negative sensations were from a current event or a memory; they were there, they hurt, and they would pass. My friends didn't need to know the details—they were there in support.

Being in the unique presence of so many people all on a similar path sharing meals, *satsang*, *asana* practice, free time and sleepy time accelerated my healing process. There was a serenity to be found in *being*, allowing the feelings to come and go, like noticing sensations as they happen in a pose—one moment your arms call your attention, then your hips or the muscles of your thighs. So, too, the pain of becoming moves around—nothing permanent, always changing.

On the YARC's last day was a wonderful *asana* practice led in turn by Tommy Rosen, Rolf Gates and Nikki Myers. Words were said that I so needed to hear: *I was sacred*. My poses were an expression of my sacred being. Never had I experienced such self-acceptance and joy in my poses. I am not the strongest, most flexible, or most expressive yoga practitioner, yet when my eyes and mind traveled off my own mat and looked around to others this time, this time I saw only other people. I did not "see a mountain as a comment on myself," just other people. That was all. My yoga practice felt just right, and I felt complete in my experience of the poses. I felt sacred, and I felt whole. Even today I hold that memory. I come back to it, and I feel just right—the right size, the right place on this earth, *right now*. With that point of reference I can identify this feeling of being sacred *any* day. I am grateful.

⸘⸙⸛

September 17: Creative Play and Hard Work

I was going to write a piece today about my challenges of facing failures; those hiccups, flawed processes, or ideas that don't pan out. These moment can make me feel as if I should give up. I then change my mind and take a break before I decide to try again. During one of these breaks I happened to see a video from this year's Burning Man (https://www.youtube.com/watch?v=cjZnCPZosOs), and I felt transformed.

My son participates in and works for that monument-burning event in Black Rock Desert, Nevada, each year. I am really proud of his dedication. I also know a little about how difficult it is, how much *tapas* (discipline) it requires to pull off an event that is filled with so much artistry, precision and fun. There is so much to be learned from an undertaking of this size. He has shared about the process over the years. Not all of the fantastic ideas for it are able to take shape in the realm of the real, but they always try, adapt, alter, change, try again, and then *do it*, at which point failure, as they say, is not an option.

The first lesson I learned from watching videos of the event, and listening to the stories of people who attended it was: *no single person does anything at this event; it takes a village to make the city.* As you view images of the installations, you can see how much cooperative play and work was required to build these amazing structures, in addition to the work of dis-assembling them from the factory or studio, carting and trucking them to Black Rock, reassembling them, enjoying them, and then either burning them up or taking them down.

The second lesson was: *they build it to let it go.* Almost every creation is unique to the event. Certainly good, enjoyable ideas are recreated from year to year, but nothing is exactly the same. The idea *and* the creative piece itself are let go; many are not only released in spirit, but also burned to the ground and all traces of them removed. Except for the videos, photos and memories, nothing remains.

The last lesson was the *wonder* of it all, the amazing respect and awe I have for the artists who create everything from marshmallow clothing to carnival-like rides and experiences, from the notes and poems written on the structures to be destroyed by fire to the engineering feats and sheer beauty of the construction. The solid-appearing buildings, the structures sporting tracery-like cut-paper art from Asia, the mobiles, and the pieces created to appear one way in the dusty day and another in the darkest desert night are all evidence of the magnificence of the creative mind, the tenacity of the creative process, and the human brain's ability to answer the question "Fun?" with a resounding *"Yes!"*

So when I eye a blank page, a lump of clay, or my yoga mat while looking for inspiration, I think, *Yes!* Yes, I can have fun. Yes, there are "do-overs." Yes, there are ways to re-imagine, re-fashion and re-do what

I have done. Yes, I can try again to learn marketing and social media, to learn how to utilize software, and to learn new computer programs. Yes, I can take a breath in these mundane tasks and ask for help from others, as the community of like-minded spirits sustain me when the tasks are hard and I feel weary. And, yes, I can let the results go, just be with what is, do the best I can, ask for help often, and then let go—wear a bizarre costume, dress up my workshop, and just *have fun.*

P.S. While whatever we look at may appear easy—a well set table and delicious meal, a well-written book, a beautiful photo, etc.—it took discipline and hard work to create these things. The Burning Man event is no different: it all looks like fun and games, but it involves a lot of people working hard on site day and night to make the event seem like effortless enjoyment.

⊱◈⊰

October 20: Like the Giant Sequoias, We Need Each Other

The sequoias are mammoth trees, soaring hundreds of feet in height with amazingly large trunks and suitably thick bark. The tallest is 275 feet high and over 2,000 years old. What is surprising is their shallow root system—barely a yard deep. These trees have no taproot and rely on a widespread web of roots. They grow in a stand or a grove, and each tree's root system is entwined in that of its sister, so that each tree supports the girth and height of another. It is their community that allows them to grow and endure. This is a marvelous picture to me: what is seen is the towering majesty of each tree, and what is unseen is the network of roots and intertwining growth beneath the soil that allows each tree to prosper.

This is how we develop in recovery programs. We cannot do it alone. We require community—a healthy healing community—to gather and share strength. We all reach the same direction: the trees to the sky, and we to recovery. It is the essence of the First Tradition: "Our common welfare should come first; personal recovery depends upon AA unity." Yes, with the companionship and strength of others in the program I am able to grow and thrive. The larger trees next to me need me as I need them, and I pass on my strength and burgeoning awareness to the new sprouts in the stand that are beginning to grow.

❧

November 12: Navigation and Finding Balance

I have just returned from the third YARC in beautiful Esalen where the redwoods meet the ocean in northern California. This center hosts personal retreats and a number of weekend and week-long retreats throughout the year. Home to wonderful organic gardens, meadows and paths to the sea, it also has the most spectacular natural hot tubs from ancient sulphur hot springs.

While relaxing in the cliffside tubs, several of us gazed skyward to see a string of over 30 brown pelicans flying along the Big Sur coast. They hugged the ragged cliffs, adjusting and adapting their path, flapping as needed to stay in line, sometimes drafting off of one another, sometimes peeling off on their own, flying, coasting, moving in and out of line, but still going in a single direction in a common quest: to seek their afternoon meal. Their choreography was beautiful, and the silent communication among the birds was wonderful to behold. The motion of the birds was similar to how the week was progressing at the conference: finding unity, finding self, drafting in the wake of someone, other times flying on one's own.

The dialogues at this YARC had moments that were more tender, and sometimes more raw, than ever before. Over half of the attendees were new, many were new to recovery, and others had returned from prior years. Some were just figuring this sobriety thing out, and a number were investigating yet deeper layers of awakening. We got to know one another, our struggles and our successes, our bravery and challenges. Many shared their new forms of play, such as slack-line (how brave and centered!), Hula-hooping (harder than it looked), and music so tender it cracked the heart wide open. The leaders (Tommy Rosen, Rolf Gates, and Nikki Myers) were right there, holding space, giving whatever was needed to help us all find our edges and be safe. The yoga practices were phenomenal, and the discourse was enlightening and helpful. I left there once again in awe of my fellow travelers.

As I returned home, I contemplated once again where I was in the "great scheme of things," both in my life and in my direction as it related to my work with others. I felt like a salad tossed aloft and then returned to the bowl with the ingredients in a different order than when freshly layered. Nikki Myers talked about the idea of maintaining true flight, secure direction and steady path, suggesting that the appearance of being on a sure-path trajectory is an illusion. In fact, we are constantly making adjustments. As a pilot constantly readjusts the path of a plane as it heads to a specific destination, our path is not set. Wind, weather, and other aircraft all have an influence on the plane's path, so adjustments to it must be made, some microscopic, others more grand. I am now more aware of the adjustments I am making as I incorporate the experiences of the last week into my evolving future.

⤳⤳

November 25: Raising the Internet—in a Positive Way

My Internet post feeds have been so positive and loving the past week or so, filled with images and quotes, videos and music all about gratitude, signs of how the Thanksgiving holiday encourages us to revisit our blessings. These posts and commentaries are certainly a vast improvement over the often acerbic comments prevalent during the past election season, as well as the oft-rampant complaints about issues of personal concern. Bad news and bad attitudes can be enticing, like an accident on the road begging to be seen: "How bad is it," "Is it someone I know?" "Is it really awful?" etc. On the Internet, "none of my business" is the best response for me.

Life In Bite-Sized Morsels

I remain positive by restricting my responses and posts to a more neutral tone, remaining focused on the solution and loving kindness, avoiding disruptive notes that can often lead to misunderstandings or negative streams of comments. I adapt the olden adage, "If you can't say something nice, don't say anything at all." Truly, I avoid jumping into a thread if all I can offer is a reinforcement of a negative or a comment of contrary substance. I scroll right by and leave the commentator and the commenters alone. I move on to seek true, inspiring, and hopeful writings from people who are reaching out for support and comfort. *That* is where I look to spend my time.

Indeed, following and posting on the positive has helped the overall tone of my Internet viewing experience. Could my clicks on the uplifting stories, the videos of courage and strength, the collection of photos about people who have performed acts of kindness, and the reports about ordinary people who have done the extraordinary be driving the news that comes to my browser? Am I teaching my search engines to present the best the Internet has to offer, rather than the gun toting worst? I enjoy reading and hearing uplifting posts and responses to life, which are signs that the Internet spiders are feeding me with more and more goodness each day. This counterbalances the pain, darkness and sadness I hear about and see.

I don't avoid the news. I don't dodge learning about the social and political ills of our time. I hear, read and see it all around me. But when the amount of discord overwhelms me and I can do nothing about it, I have to dial it down. I am also not interested in people's posts about personal anger and aggression, reading rants, and unhealthy ways of looking at one another. Posts that decry, defile and deride other people have no purpose in my brainpan. I need to look away.

There is another personal reason I veer to the uplifting and away from the oppressive. I find that positive outlooks can help me move away from my depths of discomfort. I can read about another way to look at something or a healthier way to deal with the negative. I look to my Internet community not so much to commiserate, but to coach me on my wellness journey. And I aim to do the same. It could be easier for me to find posts, news and social media that support my feelings of hopelessness and fear. Though I can find lots of validation for my bad feelings, it is a practice for me to find the positive to counteract the depressive. When I do this, I teach the Internet what to focus on and what to provide me. In this way I am raising the Internet together with others who do the same, like anonymous online parents.

Our typed words, our cyber-searches, the sites we linger on and those we breeze through all contribute to the character of this organic electronic animal. Tiffany Shlain addresses this issue in her November 2012 column in the "Flaming Brains" section of the Harvard Business Review website. She references the book *Net Smart*, in which author Robert Rheingold examines the relationship between how we humans learn and how, by extrapolation, the Internet offers us information. It turns out that what we spend time on reflects who we are, and who we are directs the Internet how to respond to us.

Shlain has created numerous videos about neurology and the Internet, drawing useful parallels between the two. She shows how we as individuals influence what is on the Internet and how the Internet influences us in return ("Brain Power: From Neurons to Networks," 2012). So I go out there today and post loving, fun, educational and playful content on the Internet and move away from the negative *samskara* (habits of the mind) that are so useless and damaging; my hope is that this will influence others to do the same.

❧

April 26: Six Observations on Losing My Voice

When you lose your voice, you can't express yourself, people can't hear you, you are stuck in your thoughts, and after a time in this isolation, you may doubt you have anything to offer.

I was on vacation with friends recently and caught a cold that took away both my hearing and my voice. I woke up deaf and silent, my body swollen with the virus, not knowing how long it would last. Communication was sparse, and yet I wanted to be included in the group.

I tried different strategies to fit in. I kept close watch on people's eyes to see the angle and persistence of their gazes. I watched their faces closely to gain information as to whom they were addressing. I was trying to figure out if my participation were requested. If I was spoken to, I tried to lip-read, to catch clues from our activity (eating, walking to the car, pointing out sights along the walk, etc.) to discern what the topic of conversation was. If indeed a response or comment was merited, I had to measure my reply carefully to mete out a loud whisper and give the briefest of answers. It was a pain for all.

The next day my hearing improved somewhat, but my voice was still limited. This became more frustrating as time went on, especially when my friends had to speak louder and more directly so I could hear them. If I talked, they had to listen to my croaky, whispery voice. This talking used a lot of energy, and my body became sore with the effort.

I learned several things as the sinus infection and laryngitis continued:

1. When my hearing was limited, I had to listen to and watch people with ferociously unwavering attention if I were to be included in the conversation. Contributing to discussions was not a spontaneous event, but a planned and measured one for me.

2. I could tell from the stillness among my friends that I was not filling the voids by merely making mouth-sounds and observations. I was not greasing the social wheel. Without my participation there was a lot of gazing and silence when we walked and at meals.

3. I lost track of my connection with others and began to feel isolated. I was but an observer, an outsider looking for the opportunity to jump in. When effort and thoughts fluctuated, I found it easier to remain silent and let my attention flag.

4. Meditation and silence as a choice are far different from experiencing quiet through unchosen hardness of hearing and inability to communicate at will.

5. My connection with my higher power was adversely affected by my thoughts turning inward and sour, because I was not as hopeful, not as filled with good humor as I usually am.

6. I lost my ability or desire to write. The isolation and struggle to remain included got me to a place where I felt I had nothing to offer, which stilled my creative voice. After a few notes and a couple of lines, my mind would wander and self-criticism would set in.

As my ears and throat cleared, my fuzzy thinking dissipated, and I was included in conversations easily once again. I did notice that my focus on my thoughts during my "deaf-mute" days made me more aware of them now. Even while I was jumping into conversations with more ease, I was asking myself: Are my thoughts useful? Is expressing them helpful? What are the unimportant vocalizations of social interaction? What contributions are necessary? How do I contribute in a positive way? During my illness-imposed silences, if conversations veered to the negative, I could throttle back my attention and cease my participation. Was that honest? If the talk was about subjects I had little interest in, I could let my mind wander. Was that rude? When I felt tired and wanted to disengage, I could do so without concern. Why could I not do that now?

This experience yielded benefits for me, but I had to work for them. I had to listen hard to see if this was an "opt in" or "opt out" type of discussion. I had time to watch my thinking and hear inside my head what was kind, harmful, useful, or detrimental. I could see where I was being judgmental rather than discerning, and supportive rather than slanderous.

I also learned a lot about gratitude, assumptions and expectations. I realize that when I listen to people I make assumptions about what they are going to say, and if I listen just a little longer, they may surprise me. (Or at least I will have listened to them rather than run them over with my words.) And I had expectations about what life would be like with a hearing deficit or the inability to speak freely. It turned out not to be as romantic, unfettered or carefree as I had surmised. Yes, I walked around with a small smile on my lips, preferring to be thought pleasant or dim rather than angry. I would look at people with an expectant gaze rather than stare away in disregard. I was able to avoid negative discourse when my hearing was impaired but I missed the community of conversation and the sounds of nature around me.

I learned a lot through that process and I am grateful to have "all my faculties intact" now. Gratitude mixed with grace.

❧

August 9: Community Will Lift and Sustain You, In the Rooms and On the Mat

I spoke with a woman yesterday whose son has been clean and sober for nearly half a year. Her relief and pride were palpable. He is safe, he is well, but for his own continued well-being he must live 3,000 miles from the temptations of drugs in his home community for now. He lives away to stay close to to a new community in recovery. After all, he needs a posse to help him sustain his sobriety.

This kind woman conveyed to me the effect her son's addictions had on his family: pain, fear, confusion. His younger brothers and sisters didn't understand why he couldn't "get better" at home, why their own care and concern for him were not enough, why he had to go so far away to heal. His parents resented their inability to be the ones to protect their child from the social sickness that resulted in his disease. They struggled with the pain of accepting that fact: in order to keep him, they had to let him go.

Just as this young man had to find a community for wellness and healing, his family needed community, too. For they were all were players in their son's unfolding drama of addiction. Their roles need to be examined, and their brain changes from being co-addicts untangled, evaluated and made well again. This cannot be done alone, nor exclusively within the family. They need a supportive community to learn and adapt the recovery tools and processes and the dispassionate perspective on the disease they need for recovery.

This woman finally related to me how powerful yoga had been for her to access and reconnect with her feelings. She had been rediscovering herself in her breath and on the mat. The yoga community was a part of the circle that lifted her up, not through advice or comments, but by listening and being witness. Yoga, along with family support systems and groups, have been helping heal her body, mind and spirit, leading her to reclaim her internal wisdom and health.

I felt for her, but also embraced her remedy: be with the wise healing community. We shared stories of pain and recovery in yoga studios, addiction recovery programs and recovery circles of all kinds. In yoga we move the trauma out of the body and breathe in wellness. Healing self will heal the family, one breath at a time.

FAMILY:
Those Closest to Us Teach Us the Most

MANY OF US feel discomfort when we think about our families, which is particularly true when we begin recovery. Whether we are recovering from a gambling addiction, debt, sex/love or substance abuse, our situations have affected our families. While the agony many change in intensity the longer I have remained in continuous sobriety, the shadows of these feelings have remained for me. Whether a specter of past guilt arises when I am feeling unbalanced or blue, or whether I am rocked back on my heels in amazement by what fine people my children have become, there is always the comparison in my heart between how I had raised them during my addiction and how I imagine I would have been as a parent had I not had this disease.

My pain, or my nostalgia, is based on an illusion: the dream that I would have been better in all ways always without the addiction. It took me many years to become a stable, thoughtful woman with healthy boundaries. I don't know if the woman I am now would have been achievable then. Nor does it matter. The lesson is that I have learned to be a better spouse, mother and daughter through the years, as well as a better niece, sister and cousin. I look on this change with immense gratitude, as often as I can I steer my mind away from the shoals of guilt and shame and into the free-flowing stream of the present moment, enjoying my family today.

I have not always been comfortable with healthy family relationships. I was used to strife, manipulation, drama and make-believe in family interactions. In early recovery, I hung out with others in recovery but was not exposed to many families who were not involved in some phase of recovery. I was also not yet comfortable with people in long-term sobriety; I hung with the younger crowd, and we were all working this sobriety thing out together. We all had strange upbringings and difficult relationships with our parents and family, and had much work to do to heal our relationships with spouses and children. The Adult Children of Alcoholics and Al-Anon programs helped me to work out the kinks of the past and develop the boundaries and self-regard essential to nurturing healthy relationships with others. This took time.

Eventually I was exposed to other types of families in my work through friends I made in these groups. I met those whose lives had not been bedeviled with active substance addiction. I met others whose knowledge of addiction was remote, e.g., a long-lost uncle or a sister-in-law. Still others had behavioral issues that had not yet impinged on their quality of life or had not percolated to the surface for examination: the smoker, the overeater, the person who craved bad news and the negative in life. I met people who didn't have a clue one way or the other because television was their sole source of information on the subject.

I am still astonished by families who don't have addiction as a centerpiece to all functions, either in action or in remediation. My husband came from one of these, and I was so uncomfortable around his friends and family I felt physically ill, developed tremors, and became hysterical on occasion just thinking about being in their company. My feeling of being "damaged goods" and fears about what they would think of me became overwhelming. I was not sure how to share; I certainly couldn't say anything about my past except to prevaricate or lie, and I didn't yet have the social skills to continually redirect the conversation back to them.

A while later there were situations I could tolerate: a brief dinner at an informal restaurant with my husband's friends, or an evening at their house, etc. His family, however, lived in another state, which meant a visit or two or more days, from which I wouldn't be able to escape, to be by myself, to scream! While I could pop out to a meeting from time to time, that involved organization of transport and an explanation I was initially unprepared to make. Just hanging around the house was difficult. I felt such pain at watching normal relations between family members, relations I had never had with my parents and siblings but had pined for. I knew intellectually that his closeness with them had not been born in the moment but from years of shared activities and traditions. I wondered if it would ever happen for me. I felt I would never be a part of it.

Time has passed. Things have changed. I have become more comfortable in my sober self and have found ways to authentically participate in family events and gatherings. They know more about me and respect my recovery; in fact, I have occasionally contributed to their understanding of the disease. With the years new chapters of family events and activities have been written, and I am on those pages, in those photos, and part of the memories. With patience on both our parts, I am part of the family now.

My relationship with my children has also taken time to mend. Rather than coming from the ineffectual stance of guilt, I needed let go of what they thought of me as the driver for my decisions, create some boundaries, and hold to them. My poor children had been such poppers on the whip end of my disease—wherever I slashed through life, they were the on the violent snap of my actions. Then I tried to fit the saccharine idea of motherhood into my child-rearing wherever I could. With the help of my counselor and the 12 Steps I found my way to becoming a genuine mother. To my great pleasure and surprise, my children have become wonderful adults—smart and creative, with self-esteem and curiosity for continued growth.

The following pieces are from various forms of exploration of my changing relationships with family and friends.

⸜❧⸝

July 14: Change and Impermanence: "It's Only Art"
When I was still actively using drugs, my children were young, and I was one of those moms rushing from childcare and preschool to work and

to college. I initially made my trips by bus, and then I got a car—a new freedom! I could go places more rapidly, therefore leave places later and schedule errands closer together. Which meant I was always in a rush. One day, while picking my daughter up from school, I put her tiny backpack and papers on the roof of my car, snapped the younger child into his car seat, jumped into the driver's side and took off. The thump of her backpack as it flew to the ground alerted me to my mistake, and I saw her papers fly off behind me as I merged into traffic. Distraught at having made yet another thoughtless error, I apologized profusely to my daughter for losing her paintings. She leaned forward, put her tiny hand on my shoulder, and said, "Don't worry, Mommy. It's only art. I'll make more."

I was in Seattle recently and visited the outdoor sculpture garden with some dear family members, my sister in-law and brother in-law. The day was spectacular, the weather perfect, and the company relaxing and amiable. While walking with them, feeling at ease, I could not help but cast my mind back to when I had first met my husband's family many years ago. I was several years into recovery but still not yet comfortable with myself. I was also not used to being in the presence of non-addicts. Up until that time most of my friends were in the program, and we all had recovery as a common bond, so I knew how to get along with them. Whether we have known each other for a long time or not, closeness comes easily with people you meet in the program, but this was not the case when I was with "normies" or "earth people." I was not used to practicing social niceties with folks who had not experienced my challenges.

The initial family events with my in-laws were at holidays. We traveled to see them, and the visit was one of days rather than hours, which made me very uncomfortable, as I was psychically unprepared to be with healthy people for extended periods of time. I would retreat to the back yard or a quiet room from time to time to get ahold of myself. Even though these were charming, welcoming, kind people, I felt nervous around them. By contrast, I came from a highly anxious family who didn't congregate for long. Over time I adjusted to my in-law family's consideration, lack of drama, and acceptance of me as I am.

Fast-forward many years, and I was in a different family constellation: a visit with my in-laws without my husband. I was walking around Seattle with them on my own. I was in a new pond, building a new way to communicate. I was getting to know true family, a closeness evolving on a very different level and rate of intimacy. And I was comfortable with that. We talked about everything and anything. We were together for half a day, and the time flew. It was wonderful evidence that things change.

From the outdoor garden we moved into the visitors' center, where we saw an exhibit of boats and water scenes. At the entrance was a humongous painting of a boat on turbulent waves a team of artists had applied directly to the wall with Sharpies, adding silver and white paint to create beautiful waves and designs evocative of Japanese ocean paintings. We read the description of the work and discovered that in a year it was to be painted over. Something else would take its place. This planned change and acceptance of impermanence mirrored the words my daughter had expressed: "Don't worry, Mommy. It's only art. I will make more."

Yes, feelings change, relationships change, and, evidently, art changes. Nothing is permanent, not even the beautiful and good—but particularly not the uncomfortable and difficult. I thought about how I had changed over the years, how my relationships had developed. Graced as I am for the present moment, I remain open to change. And this awareness is available to me because I abstained from drink and drugs, one day at a time, and have done so for many years. So don't quit five minutes before the miracle, because things change. You will, too.

❦

August 14: Zombies, Safety and a Mother's Love

A few months ago I was talking to my daughter on the phone. She is the mom (and I the proud grandmother) of three boys aged 14, 9, and 5. As we were talking, the youngest was preparing to go outside and play. They live in a small seaside town in northern California, and "outside" means into the yard, meadow and woods. His current fashion preference has been shorts, and that day he was wearing surfer-style swim trunks held up by a drawstring. As he was getting ready to go out, he insisted that certain accessories be tied to the drawstring: a tuning fork, a set of keys, and the tiny, sword-like plastic handle one uses in a tray to make Popsicles. My daughter asked him what he was going to do with those things. He proudly announced that he was going outside to "kill zombies."

Once we stopped laughing about his attire, I asked about the "killing" and the "zombies." I know the undead are very popular in mainstream culture, and I was curious as to how this had become his mission. She related the story to me in a way that demonstrated how she (unlike *her* mother) exhibited patience, restraint, and understanding:

The previous night her youngest son had been home alone with his older brothers, who were not "allowed" to watch or play scary movies or video games in front of the impressionable tot. When they did view this genre when the parents were home their little brother would be removed from the room and distracted with another activity. But that seemed to have left their minds while Mom and Dad were away, so the 5-year-old got an eyeful and brainful of zombie wars. He was so scared he decided to "get into the solution" and take matters into his own hands. The next day, arming himself with those three implements, he went out to clear the area around the house of zombies and make it safe for his family. My daughter saw this and understood. She didn't worry about losing the tuning fork or one of a set of six Popsicle handles, nor did she try to explain to him that the zombies weren't "real" and he had nothing to fear. She gave him the dignity of his solution and let him go out to slay zombies.

Acknowledging in some childlike way what he felt and thought, he would go outside, fix things, and then wouldn't feel so afraid. Would that we all were "Mom" to ourselves, supporting and arming ourselves to surmount our own inner fears. Would that we could all find solutions and permit ourselves to vanquish what caused us to be afraid with no judgment about the form or fashion: useful tools or ones with imaginary powers, dressed in battle armor or Bermudas, discovering ways to keep ourselves safe.

Taking these thoughts into meditation and then to the mat, today I will face a pose I don't care for, or am afraid of trying. Today I will sit with what causes me discomfort. Today I will look around me and find the tuning fork, the keys and the Popsicle handle and carry them with me so that I might not be so afraid. I thank my grandson for giving me a way to handle the zombies in my mind.

⤸⤹

July 28: Family and Friends "Discount"

A yummy summer treat! My daughter's children are coming to stay with us for a few days next week. I so look forward to this special time with them. The three boys will all be here for several overnights without their parents—the first time for the youngest, who is five. I have ideas about what we can do and see, excursion for fun, trips for education, ways to entertain and amuse us all.

I am also looking for balance between companionship in the home, just being together, home projects, things to do outdoors, and going to museums and parks. Thinking and planning: so far, so good. I overlay my ideas with my current work schedule. My planning and excitement and the desire to do lots with the boys begins to look like *busy, busy, busy, busy*—not the way I want to run my life, and not the way I want to experience their visit. I am too excited. Back to balance.

Now to put a plan in place. Having my list of events and looking at my calendar, I evaluate how I can fit the puzzle-pieces of activity into the schedule. Uh-oh—I teach, I have meetings with people, I have commitments. Hubby can pick them up, and their arrival will dovetail with the appointments I have that day. For the next day I will schedule excursions for the boys around the classes on my agenda, and then I will return home and make arrangements for dinner and so on through the days they are here. I am now in the space of rushing (in my mind), my breath becomes short, I feel anxious, and my heart gets heavy.

I take a breath and consider what I am holding on to—those ropes of attachment I won't release. Why am I hell-bent on constant business? What are some appointments I can let go? Why won't I? I ask myself, "What are the strings that bind you so tightly to activity? Why are you gripping to the ponderous planning?"

My heart gets heavy, because memories come flooding back to when I was a woman newly in recovery, a single mom with kids, going to AA meetings, working with my sponsor, managing my kids' activities and the duties of running a home. I was always scheduling stuff around other stuff, barely being present in one moment as I urgently prepared for the next one. I remember rushing my kids from here to there, seldom *being* with them just as they were. My full schedule created an emptiness in me. I now feel in danger of repeating that process with my grandkids.

As a yoga teacher and student, I practice being in the present moment rather than the next one. I am conscious of the importance of *prana*, the life force, that dissipates when the mind is in someplace other than the body. I don't fancy going back to the time of planning to do while in the midst of doing, particularly while the grandkids are here on vacation.

Discount: this word means both reduction in price and disregard for someone or something. Discount is good when applied to *cost*, but not when applied to *care*; while I love offering (and receiving) "friends and family" discount on goods and services, I never want to be the donor of disregard. Perceived or actual, I never again want to be in a position to give kids the idea that they are pawns on a game board of obligation or that their needs are subservient to my own. Rushing around gives the impression that whatever we are in the midst of doing is merely to be completed so that we move on to the next, more "important," activity. When you are a kid and the activity is *not* you or something that has to do with you, then that feeling of what is next, means you are not that important. Whatever or whoever is next is the real beneficiary of a parent's love, attention and energy. That next thing can be grocery shopping, work, or car repair—it matters not. Even though those activities are done with the children's health, security and safety in mind, the kids are being discounted in the present for this coming-up activity.

I have learned that the past need not prognosticate the future. Yes, as a single mom I needed to work, to be the logistics and supply manager of the home, and to devote myself to my sobriety. But the attitude of rush and motion was desperate, unskilled, and possibly dismissive of the children's thoughts, feelings and desires. I was not yet skilled enough to be in the moment and let go of what will or could happen next.

In the practice of my recovery principles (working the 6th and 7th Steps) and my yoga (*brahmacharya*, non-excess, and *aparigraha*, non-holding on), I can approach my complicated schedule with a calmer intention, keeping alternatives available: reduce my work schedule, find substitutes, defer meetings that can be delayed without insult or harm, and keep it simple. Let the community, not the activity, be the important part of the visit. The gift of my grandsons' presence could be the guiding factor, not the agendas or activities. I must also notice that the planning was all mine, without regard for or input about their actual interests and ideas. I will keep some options in mind, ask them and see what develops. Oh, and let the children drive the bus on occasion.

EGO AND ACCEPTANCE:
Learning to Discern the Big
"E" from the Little "e"

In RECOVERY I have learned to find my true self in the right size: neither too important, smart or skilled nor unimportant, stupid or inept. This is a true balancing act born of working the steps, studying, and listening to the wisdom of others, both one-on-one and in recovery meetings. I have had to dig deep to find out the sources of my feelings of "less than" and to investigate the reasons for my attitude of "better than."

Recovery literature repeatedly tells us that the "ego must be smashed." The 12 x 12 book reiterates the need to set aside the ego and the dangers of the self-centered ego. Humility, it is maintained, can be found only when the ego is shelved. That refers, I believe, to all qualities of the ego: the one that is too big and too much, the one that is the guest of honor at the pity party, and the one that is too small, self-centered in a meek way. Many people in addiction suffer from both simultaneously.

Because low self-esteem is problematic and typical for someone who grew up in a home with active alcoholism, it is that side of ego-focus I have suffered from. As I was growing up, I would give way to others' preferences and choices, looking to others for approval and affirmation. My feelings were tied up in the wellbeing of my family members and friends. So much time passed in this illusion of "otheration" that I felt I had lost sight of what I would like, want or need. Through working the steps of recovery I found out this was only partially true: many times I knew what I wanted and what I would choose, even when yielding to others. I would instead do the other's bidding and hold resentments toward that person, pack these resentments up, and eventually develop anger, expectations of reward, or both. I would appear to be kind and compliant when inside I was plotting revenge or some type of compensation, emotional or otherwise. It took me humility to recognize this and to change my actions and attitudes accordingly.

At times the effect of low my self-esteem was not apparent to me. I made choices about work options, friends and companions, even purchases, thinking I was not worthy of anything better. I would stay in jobs that underutilized and underpaid me, feeling this was about all I could do or was worth. I found companions when I was in active addiction who endorsed and promoted a sleazy lifestyle. I felt awkward and unworthy when I was with people who had good jobs, maintained their homes, and treated themselves and their families with respect. Particularly when I drank and used drugs, I was far more comfortable hanging out with the undershirt-clad, unshaven, beer-belching boys than go to parties where people conversed and danced while drinking. When I would buy things, I would be far more generous in my selections for others (a type of ego-feeding action) rather than myself. I would purchase expensive gifts for others while using kitchenware or bedding I found in the street for myself and family. I now know that some of these choices came from a low sense of self-worth, coupled with my need for recognition. I could excel at a job I was overqualified for, gaining accolades while I avoided challenge. I could be the beauty among the beasts and the thoughtful, unselfish one in the crowd. *All ego.*

I have grown a lot since then through practicing the principles of recovery and yoga to unearth and investigate my core ego issues. Yet the work is not complete. The ego still raises her head, and in a strange way I am grateful now when she pops up; when I experience feelings of imperiousness, braggadocio, or disdain, it means trouble and I need to investigate what is going on. Conversely, when I start feeling meek, small or lacking in self-confidence, there is also a problem requiring investigation. Both conditions help me grow—when I see them and work on them. The prospect no longer fills me with shame, but with appreciation. I look forward each day, still, to growing and finding the healthy ego—the ego of the true self.

❧

October 12: My Ego is a Pain in the Neck

I am not sure this is how it happened, but most likely it was something I did to myself. About ten days ago I got it into my head to go into my garage-studio and throw big pieces: a large bowl, plate or vase. (I am a potter, so by "throw big pieces" I mean that I was going to throw, or create, pots on my potter's wheel with greater amounts of clay than usual.) I did so for two days, wedging, centering and throwing 8 to 10 pounds of clay, making several pieces in a row, for a few hours at a time. I would leave the studio to teach my yoga classes, and in the few evenings I had at home I knitted.

Add to that my screen time and there was a lot of "favoritism" on my right side, with my head suspended over my right shoulder. *Voilà*—the magic mixture of overdoing in many areas ended in a weird neck pain with negative nerve messages going from scalp to wrist, accompanied by large knots in my shoulder and neck muscles. But, hey, I am a yoga teacher! I know what to do! I just use small massage balls, do a few stretches, and right as rain...NOT! I actually had to get professional help, in the form of a chiropractor.

To support his readjustment work, I began to reduce my monitor time, my mat efforts, and my other activities. I had to—I could neither rotate my head nor lift my arm above my shoulder! Acceptance and humility put me in a position where my physical limitation needed to be honored. I teach classes with reduced range of motion, operating within my capacity when demonstrating poses. Restricted movement contains a hidden surprise—I am modeling what I teach: "Work within your capacity, and use your breath to discover what that is." Pain will make you gasp, and there is little if no gasping in yoga.

With contrast therapy (ice, then heat), reduced activities, and household help from hubby, I am back on the road to mobility, as long as I continue to practice moderation. I have to care for myself as I would want you to care for yourself. I feel better, now that I mindfully continue to throttle back activities so I don't overdo them. I am prone to overdoing. *That* is how I got into this mess.

⚜

February 19: Yoga, Service, and Self-Expression

I am still stoked about being interviewed for Rob Schware's column. So many people are taking their yoga service and practices to worthy groups—veterans, the disabled, the mentally challenges, those enduring suffering of all types. I am happy to have my work included among them. As an advocate for yoga's benefits, Schware does a fabulous job of bringing to light the variety of ways we are called to support one another through yoga. His column provides a type of advocacy that expands the public's view of what yoga really is. One can discover that it is more than poses, more than the physical challenge of an expanding practice. It is not gymnastics and exercise. Yoga is a way of being in the world and looking at the world. Service can provide a huge piece of the balance we look for in our lives. Rob Schware allows us to read about all manners and types of service and to be part of a large community of benevolent practitioners.

I want to promote his *Huffington Post* column. I am also proud to be part of it. Yet I am also shy about sharing it. Yes, it is about service, and yes it may help the reader find help and possibly more columns about more types of service. The column may entice the reader to participate in healing, sharing and/or giving. But really, I want you to read about me and my work. It may be immodest of me to wish for the reader to investigate and possibly use my services, but I also know that to benefit from my work you must be able to find me. This is the part of "ego" I struggle with. Self-promotion is immodest. I believe in what I do, and I believe it is useful. But how do you get the word out about your services without sounding like you are bragging?

I was listening to a *Forum* program on NPR, February 19, 2013, about bragging: bragging about our kids, oneself, the public posts we put on Facebook, etc. Authors and professionals discussed people's impressions of the ways we present ourselves to those we know and those we don't know. They presented criteria for distinguishing a useful "brag" from an annoying bout of self-aggrandizement, or gloating about our kids or pets. (The interview can be found at http://www.huffingtonpost.com/rob-schware/service-yoga_b_2578785.html.)

Our relationship with others determines what is viewed as bragging and what is not. The difference lies in how people respond to personal information based upon how much they know about us. Do they know our trials and tribulations, so that the successes we share are part of a broader landscape about ourselves? Do they feel invested in the whole of our lives, or are these bulletins of derring-do just more of the *"It's All About Me!"* advertisement we are putting out there? So when I share, am I confident that you know the struggles of recovery, to know my journey from addict to yogi in service? Or am I in danger of having my information seen as bragging or boasting? It is a challenge to know what is useful and what is noise.

(The interview can be found at http://www.huffingtonpost.com/rob-schware/service-yoga_b_2578785.html.)

❧

March 2: Comparing Myself to Others: Eating Appropriately

I love vegetables. Just standing at the counter with a pile of freshly rinsed veggies and my favorite knife can be bliss for me. I look at their color and smell the bright splash of scent when I put in the first cut. A bit later, I have piles of chopped bits of this, slices of that, and torn shreds of another item. The colors intrigue me, and I feel happy.

Then the stress arrives. According to some input based on my *dosha* (my constitution and condition), I should not eat vegetables raw.

Life In Bite-Sized Morsels

According to others, I should eat only uncooked vegetables. Additional sources scorn fruits, while others propose that half of what I eat be leafy greens. I should cleanse my body periodically; I should purify and remove the need for cleansing. I should buy special foods and supplements; I am not treating my body as I should. The input on what "special foods" and "supplements" are varies from year to year, study to study, and passionate person to passionate person. What should I do?

The cost of special foods concerns me. I look at the pile on the counter and wonder: where *did* this come from? What season is it? What would be growing in this area now? If it didn't grow here, where *was* it grown? I want affordable food, but what is the real, actual, full cost of my organic, out-of-season fruits and vegetables? How "special" am I that my all-green, close-to-the-sun, raw, organically grown, barely affordable food should cost the planet human, transportation and other unseen costs to get me my salad in the dead of winter?

And I do worry about the planet. I think about the need to eat with the season. This would reduce import, environmental and transportation costs and keep local farmers in business. Yet if I did go seasonal, I would not have the majority of the vegetables that are glistening on the counter. Right now the root vegetables are plentiful. I love them. Eating them, however, violates many nutrition rules: They are not grown on vines or stalks; they don't grow up near the sun; if not organic, they are the ones that absorb most of the toxins used in many farms. The fertilizer goes into the soil, where these tubers flourish.

Which rule *do* I violate to feed this body? The local-farm-fresh rule? The near-the-sun rule? The raw rule? The organic rule? I look to others, the nutrition counselors, as I am confused. Which only brings more confusion—they don't all agree. Some suggest raw and extracted. (No fiber?) Another advised doing a cleansing—get all the toxins out! (Then what?) Still others suggest eating as ancient prehistoric man did. My mind swells in frustration. *Back to basics,* I say. *Brahmacharya* in this as well—non-greed and non-excess. What if I did some, not all, of what was suggested? What if I were moderate in my selections and just did my best? I currently choose tri-color eating: three different colors of food at each meal. (Shades of beige don't count.)

Part of my concern comes from thinking about what non-bourgeois, non-middle class, non selfied people do. How can people on fixed and minimum-wage incomes afford to eat fresh food in this major metropolitan area? Without a healthy, well-rounded diet, we need vitamins, so we sometimes take supplements despite a healthy diet. Most Americans cannot buy supplements to augment certain food choices. Food stamps and SNAP (Supplemental Nutrition Assistance Program) do not cover vitamins, although they do cover chips and candy. Magazines will sometimes run articles on how to eat for pennies a day, but they more often have articles on how to give yourself spa treatments from the kitchen: applying avocados to your face and hair, and other food products to your feet and hands. Most people don't have enough money to eat much less so they can rinse and massage themselves with organic food. (If they had it, they would eat it.)

I am actually lucky to have these concerns about what season to eat from, and how to prepare my abundant sources of food so I can have all food groups within not just a day, but in one meal! I am also lucky I can entertain the illusion that eating food in a certain way will allow me to become the slim-hipped, narrow-waisted woman the media depict as healthy.

I am forgetting the primary purposes of food: to nourish and, if I am lucky enough, to be shared as the communion of friendship manifested in a meal—nothing more, not a source of pride or comparison, not a place to go to harm my sense of self, not another way to sabotage my self-care and self-esteem. These worries over food, the best way to prepare it, what to combine, what supplements to use, etc., are the luxuries of the "haves." By letting go of the ego of the kale food group acolytes, I refocus my concern to the "have-nots." Rather than letting myself be bullied by the overbearing attitudes and opinions of the nutritional elite, I refocus on being grateful for my food, eating a reasonable amount, and letting go of wanting to be part of the juicers.

Who with strong opinions about the preparation and type of food can shop for a family of four in the healthiest way with food stamps or SNAP? I have been reading about groups and communities trying to do just that. I did it for three years when on welfare, trying to feed my children well with the most meager of resources. (Feeling brave? Try the food stamp challenge and share your successes and challenges with others. Maybe together with this experience we can authentically help others who don't have enough to eat.)

What do I do now? Back to the old cutting board. I proceed to prepare dinner. Some of these lovelies are for a delicious salad—yes, raw—and some are going into veggie lasagna—yes, cooked; yes, sauce from a jar (but a really good brand); yes, with dairy products, and layering it all with whole-wheat noodles, because I am nothing if not a "natural" cook.

My food should not bring stress. It should not reduce my sense of self-esteem (comparing to others is toxic, remember). It should not cause me to feel like I'm failing my body. I also don't want to feel like I'm taking more than my share of the world's resources, or behaving in a way that can harm others. So I do what I can, and let go of the results. *Bon appétit!*

❧

April 13: Vanity, Humility, and Just Getting Over It

OK, I admit it. I have feelings of vanity. I want to let go of the hopes of a perfect image of my physical self. I struggle with that a lot. I say this not to get the response of "You have nothing to worry about!", "You look great for your age" or any other reply of reassurance. I say this merely as an observation. This struggle with vanity was something I encountered when I started a new project: recording recovery yoga classes. Allowing myself to be videoed required a whole new level of rational self-acceptance.

But I didn't feel rational. I was worried about how I would look, how I would sound, the appearance and limitations of my practice, and so on. I then turned those doubts into stage fright: *What if I froze? What if I forget what I'm doing? What if I'm no good?*

Then I flip into the desire to practice humility. First, though, I didn't find humility—only useless self-undersizing: I started to feel too small, too insignificant, not as accomplished as those I admire. I am not like Nikki Myers, Rolf Gates, Tommy Rosen, or B.K. Bose, the pantheon of amazing yoga personalities and service workers. "Who am I to do this?" is a limiting belief, but I felt it. This kind of thinking, like vanity, is all about me and totally useless when it comes to creating an offering for others. My videos were designed to be helpful to others. *That* was the point of the project—not to be a "star."

So what did I do? I made them! I found that sweet space between doing it to bolster my ego and feeling too small to try it. I moved back to my desire to be of service, for neither false vanity nor perseverating about being unworthy would fulfill my mission. In fact, both vanity and false humility bring the focus on me rather than the classes, which are all about the student.

The classes were recorded in order that anyone could view them at any time. I designed them for the person in recovery, using recovery concepts with focus on healing, hoping the videos could be part of the tools used to care for oneself, a positive practice to change the negative *samskara* (habits) of the mind, to convert negative brain chatter into positive phrases and recovery-oriented concepts. Every class was designed to remind you that you are complete as you are, to love yourself as you are, and to know you have space and safety to grow in a healthy way. These are lessons I have learned along the way, and re-learned in the process of making the videos.

After this back-and-forth in my mind—being apprehensive about my body and voice, my practice and presentation—I dropped the rock of my worries, got on my mat, and took my teachings to heart. I included in my prayer the intention to know that I am just the right size, my practice is authentic, I won't hurt myself, and my pose-cueing words are kind. I listened and allowed the process to unfold, ever true to myself and my recovery. I overcame my vanity, found humility in the right amount, and just got over it—for hiding behind vanity was an exercise in vain.

❦

August 29: Being Public Invites the Ego: The Gratitude Challenge

I am in the middle of an online "Gratitude Challenge," a form of public declaration of gratitude. You join the challenge by being named by someone having just completed the process. You then pick up the challenge and complete it yourself by posting three things a day for a number of days. At the end, you nominate three more people to continue with the challenge process.

At first I liked the idea of posting all of these positive statements on the Internet, as a cosmic positive daily list to offset the negativity that can crop up online. When I first participated, I was lighthearted and excited about it. I read other people's lists, and they were similar to mine: most cheerful, some whimsical. Then postings began to get serious: lists were more "profound" and "heavy." Wanting to "be part of" that, I followed suit. Each posting about gratitude was weighed down with philosophical gravitas, becoming more and more ponderous each day.

Subsequent "nominations" to the gratitude challenge were becoming less fun as a result. I became aware of a shift in my sense of gratitude, how I would express it, and what I wanted to put out there in public. I, too, wanted my gratefulness to have weight and substance, to reflect the deep sense of thankfulness I have for my sobriety and all life has offered me: recovery, health, family, friends, home group, my yoga practice, my students and clients, etc. The genuine gratitudes I find in my life are small: remembering to make a call I had forgotten to write down, catching a glass before it fell to the floor, a parking space, the an amber light, a favorite song on the radio. I have at least a dozen daily moments for which I say "Thank You" out loud, but these moments are meaningful only to me: I lose my way driving somewhere, and I am grateful for the yards and gardens I get to see that I would otherwise have missed; I check the wrong book out of the library, and I am happy for the opportunity to read something the universe had picked for me; etc. But trying to capture them and put them in sentences for public consumption was both difficult and trite. Stating them in public overwhelmed me.

After a while, what I felt compelled to post online had morphed into something different than the spontaneous outbursts of "Thank you." Like putting on my best clothes for a special visit, I wanted to pick out the best and most "public-worthy" (whatever that is) aspects of my life to place in public for my practice.

Yes, once again my ego has intervened to make a right mess of a simple process: "Just write down three things." *But people are going to read them, I think, and probably judge me, and think about how shallow I am if there are things like finding your phone under the car seat, or remembering to pick up a friend's item from the lost-and-found at the yoga studio. The public statements of gratitude must be profound.*

As the gratitude challenge has become the ALS Ice Bucket of Internet postings, reading the lists of others also has less of an effect on me. I used to read each one with relish, as most started out simple, silly, fun and light. But even for them, once the subjects of recovery, family, and friends were exhausted, those posts, too, often became heavy and esoteric.

When nominated to pick up the challenge, I would feel churlish if I didn't follow up, even though I am enjoying it less. But now, having investigated the effect of my ego on the process, I think I will get off my high horse and be less fancy. So, next time you read my gratitude posts, know that I will be more honest, more realistic, and less vast—possibly silly. You have been warned!

CODEPENDENCE, BOUNDARIES AND BALANCE:
Getting Grounded Grants Freedom

DEFINING AND MAINTAINING boundaries and limits and defending my right to say "no" have been an odyssey of self-discovery and self-regard. As a single mom in my early sobriety, I was run over by my kids for a couple of years before I learned to hold a consistent line regarding behavior, chores and our relationship. There were two parts to this: (1) determining what the limits were for me, and then (2) committing to them with the children.

First, I needed to discover for myself what the true rules were, the requirements I had for comportment and for participation in the home. I had to make them clear and firm, but they needed to be age appropriate. By the time I finally figured some out, they had to be changed, for the kids had grown, and the rules needed to grow with them. Learning from the program that it is "principles, not personalities," yet keeping in mind that exceptions prove the rule, I made plenty of mistakes.

The second part was no less easy. I had to accept that my children would not always be happy with me, that I would sometimes disappoint or anger them. After years of ineffectual parenting, setting rules and limits came as quite a shock to them. They were not pleased with me. As I had begun this process when they were elementary-aged, they knew a bit about what was coming. I did not, however, develop spine until they were in their early teens. This presented a difficult challenge. I did learn about my boundaries, though: I became more skilled in understanding that the consequences, the results of their actions or inaction, were not my "fault" but theirs.

Life In Bite-Sized Morsels

I had to learn about my own limits and requirements, balance them with appropriate outcomes, and let go of how they felt about me. I wanted them to love me. I wanted a harmonious home. I wanted overt signs of mutual respect. And people in hell want ice water. I had to get over it.

Boundaries with friends and understanding my limitations were another challenge for me. I wanted to be all things to all people, and ended up being of no good to anyone. I couldn't be at work all the time pleasing my boss *and* be at home with the kids (mom on tap) for the occasions they wanted me there, much less at all games, concerts and meetings, *and* say yes to every request for service in recovery (chairing, secretary and sponsorship) *and* call my mom as frequently as she had wanted me to. Any two of these were incompatible; all of them together were a minestrone of unmet needs. I was making no one happy, and I was making myself miserable. I needed to learn to say "no." I needed to develop balance and self-care. It continues to be difficult, but I do work on it.

Part of the boundary-setting came from learning to be a "man among men," or, in my case, a "peep among people." I didn't need to be Super-Mom, Super-Worker, Super-AA-ette. The issues around ego and self-esteem needed to be addressed so that I was not wringing myself out to gain approval and acceptance. Except for health and safety emergencies, my family was my priority, so I needed to act like it. I learned to leave work in the evening at a reasonable time, to ask for time off to be with the kids in school when needed. I even scheduled vacation. I set a regular time to check in with my mom; she would know when it was, and I could contain that contact as I needed to. Limiting the number of women I sponsored had been very difficult: each one presented herself as a wonderful woman with admirable commitment to recovery. I had to say "no" so they could get the sponsor they deserved—one with sufficient time and energy. I also needed to avoid saying "yes" and volunteering whenever there was a silence. Letting others come forward was as important as my stepping back.

Once I had identified some of the big-stroke boundaries, I started to work on the finer, more discerning ones, mostly pertaining to time and rest. I set intentions rather than make resolutions or promises. I act the way I want to be treated rather than mandating that from a "rules" perspective. I used to say, "I am going to try not to do that [whatever "that" was] anymore," so I practiced removing the word "try" and simply ceased that activity rather than announcing it. When I deleted the "try"—which had given me kind of a loophole—and just made and followed the intention from inside, I was much more successful. Instead of trying not to volunteer for everything, I stopped, considered, asked questions, and then decided if I could do the job justice. *Look at ego, look at priorities, look at time, and take time, in the day, on the calendar, to rest.*

Balance is crucial. In yoga we balance in all poses, not just the special one-legged, or arms-only ones. I call it "balancing the load." In yoga poses we find a way to share the effort throughout the body. We start with the big muscles and then parse out the difficulty to other running muscles. When fatigue is felt in one group, with this discernment and experience the load can be shifted to another set of muscles. You can either hold your arms up parallel to the ground using the shoulders or use your underarms to push your arms up.

This is equally true in life. We each have strengths and sub-strengths. I am smarter and more organized in the early morning. If I have a difficult task, I prefer to schedule it then. Routine and mundane works better for me in the evening, in which laundry and housecleaning can be done. When I balance my energetic load, I evaluate the things I have to do and, when possible, spread them out along my energetic continuum. I am now more mindful of the look of my whole week and aware of how many full days I have. I then find breaks in the week and schedule them for myself, to have a pause. When the unexpected comes up, I also then have space to address it. If I schedule myself end-to-end every day in the week, I have no place to go but Hyperville if I need to get my vehicle smogged, or wait at home for a repair person, or have space to be with a friend who is in the hospital. I no longer prefer to be manic. I am finding equanimity.

Through boundaries, limit-setting and balance, I now have the possibility for greater equanimity. I love those times when I can do that, hold the line, and be effective in the undertaking. However, practicing *satya* (non-lying), I need to say it is a practice that is in no way near perfection. But, one day at a time, I "try."

⌘

December 28: Intentions and Resolutions

I learn so much from people at meetings. A month or so ago we were talking about intentions, and a woman said she "found the results of her intentions in her crisper bin." We all burst out laughing, because we all know that drawer in the fridge—the one with exotic vegetables: celery root, kale, mustard greens, varieties of eggplants large and small, wizened mushrooms and fungus, as well as the traditional salad-makings and snacking carrots. I buy them myself in a passion for healthy eating, imagining preparing new dishes and tasting new flavors. I get them all at once, not realizing there is no possible way to consume them all before they become limp, pale shadows of their previous snappy, robust selves. The worst case is they all get purchased, put away, and then forgotten until they dissolve into a hard-to-discern soup or paste. I toss them out in shame, another good idea gone bad, another set of resolutions forgotten or ignored.

Similarly I have embarked on a plan to change something, anything, in my life. This had led to the gym memberships, the facial scrubs and protocols, the potted plants, and the purchased food. Most often this desire had come from a deeper longing to feel differently, to make acceptable something I found unacceptable, or to make wholesome feeling of disintegration.

There is that moment of internal discord when I know I need to change something, get frustrated, land on the superficial, and then try to implement a plan. I start on the outer layer, the physical, and try to change everything: my looks, weight, hair, face, and skin—the obvious and external. I also try to do it all at once.

If I strive for too much too soon without really feeling my way through the process, I over-promise myself and set the path to failure, as I had done in active addiction: "I want it all now." Instead, I could get one new vegetable per week, make one small change per month, to try it on, see how it works, practice the commitment to the intention as much as the intention itself.

The next time I set an intention, I will start with an empty, clean crisper and take my time to fill it. In lieu of a resolution to eat healthier, I can bring the intention of one new vegetable a week into my life. Instead of pledging to start running again, I will take meditative walks. In making the plan to treat myself with respect, I will move in the direction of health, not appearance. Rather than making a promise, I can have a goal. I will investigate the landscape of "some" rather than looking to find happiness in "all." Here's to you, new crisper bin—may we make new friends this year.

❧

December 28: Boundaries and Freedom: The String on the Kite Gives it its Height

I am a woman recovering from many things. First to come to the surface was my chemical addiction to drugs and alcohol; I could not yet address my codependency, relationship, sexual, consumerism or food issues until I had become clean and sober. Some were obvious at various times, others were masked for years, and still others had developed along the way.

The wellspring of all of my addictive actions and behaviors stems from defenses and protective patterns I had developed as a child. My relationships with others and myself had been poisoned by maladaptive behaviors acquired and amplified by growing up in a home with an alcoholic mom and an emotionally unstable dad. I perfected these behaviors in my years of drinking and using. What *were* these unhealthy patterns? My desire to please knew no bounds—there were no lengths to which I would not go to gain acceptance, praise, and approval. I also felt as if I did not matter. While I was loved, my needs were not met. The instability of the family emotional landscape left me feeling unmoored and insubstantial. The loving did not include support on an ongoing, predictable basis. My self-esteem was low, and I had become emotionally shut-down. Like many suffering from the dis-ease of co-addiction, I had the top ten behaviors.

As the oldest child, I assumed the mantle of the "responsible one" and retain aspects of this even today, particularly when I am out of balance. I occasionally still experience feeling responsible for things that are none of my business, much less under my control. This branches out to the illusion that I am responsible for the happiness and feelings of others, when clearly this is not the case. The need to control can leak from there, so I behave like an "actor who wants to run the whole show." When younger, I truly did not feel happy unless the other members of the house were happy. When they didn't, I felt guilty. While this cycle has diminished nearly completely, I am still in awe that I should be free of its grasp.

I used to get quite defensive when criticized or corrected. It hurt so much I could almost not bear it. When stating an opinion, I would couch it in qualifying phrases and pre-stated apologies hoping I wouldn't offend anyone. Terrified of making mistakes, I would do only activities at which I was competent. I remember the first day I realized that making a mistake could be totally freeing and that the world opened up when I was willing to try new things. That memory is still takes my breath away it was so astounding.

Instant intimacy was a huge problem for me. I would reveal more about myself and my shortcomings. I think I did this both to try to make others feel more comfortable with me, and to "pre-criticize" myself so they wouldn't have to. I had no personal boundaries. If I felt like I could trust someone, regardless of situations to the contrary, I would open my heart, home and family to that person. It would take a great deal of betrayal before I realized I was being lied to, ripped off, used. This pattern became subtler in recovery, but I had a way to go before I realized I needed to set and maintain limits for myself and for others in relation to me.

Anger and loud voices can still shake me up. I am more skilled at handling my reactions, but I still do react. They are triggers for me. Violence and rage followed me from my childhood into adulthood, affecting both me and my children. I may be susceptible to the aftershocks for some time to come. Grounding, breathing, and present-time awareness help me to bring current events into the present moment and disentangle them from the past.

Investigating my relationship with others and my relationship with myself has become the theme for the recent decade of my recovery journey.

December 20: The End of the World and Living Today Fully

The Mayan Calendar is taking center-stage in online news, out of widespread concern that it does not extend past the final days of 2012, signifying the end of all beings. Many of us smile at the idea of an end to the world; however, there can be a kernel of truth in the concept. Each day is the end of, well, that day. So, in a way, the end of time was yesterday. The good news is that each subsequent day is new and ripe with opportunity.

The groups I have been meeting with on Monday and Friday nights have been sharing their wisdom and experience with yogic topics such as *tapas* (discipline/transformation) and *aparigraha* (non-attachment/non-clinging). We talk about our challenges and solutions to these dilemmas. Their words come to my mind as I center and prepare myself for each day. Allowing steadfast attention to my intentions for each day, I practice *tapas*. That keeps me in the requirements of today without putting things off to the future. This day will end, so I must fill each day with thrall for the present moment. By letting go of the past—even the recent past—and its plans, disappointments, expectations and predictions, I am open to the new day to be what it is and what it offers. It takes guts, grit, and determination to let go—that is the discipline I practice.

Exercising *aparigraha*, I also let go of how things unfold and develop. I get better and better at leaving the path of tomorrow until tomorrow. In this way, I live in today fully. I embrace the interruptions of my "plan" by the unexpected call or conversation with a student or the malfunction of a car, computer or cable connection as merely a moment in the day, not a breakdown of the "plan." I also find some bit of information, lesson or strength in adapting to that event. Knowing I am doing my best with what I have in the time I have to do it, it helps me practice for myself the compassion I have for others. While I don't live in tomorrow, I do know that what I do today lays the groundwork for what I do tomorrow, how I am, and where I am.

So whatever happens tomorrow, I am prepared for it, because I am living today fully.

⧬

July 8: Who Am I if I Let Go?
Co-Addiction and its Many Pains

The Buddha once asked a student, "If a person is struck by an arrow, is it painful?" The student replied, "It is." The Buddha then asked, "If the person is struck by a second arrow, is that even more painful?" The student replied again, "It is." The Buddha then explained, "In life, we cannot always control the first arrow. However, the second arrow is our reaction to the first. *The second arrow is optional.*"

What are *your* arrows? One of my first arrows was having been born into a family with an alcoholic parent and the other suffering from mental issues. For many, the first arrow was living with the active addiction or the relapse of a loved one. That is so painful. Living with someone who can turn from being a bright, vivacious, entertaining, loving and funny person into someone dark, maudlin, untrustworthy, self-absorbed and dangerous is painful. The lies, the deception, the hiding, the worry, and the guilt all amount to making every waking moment difficult. This is the life of the co-addict. This is the first arrow.

The second arrow comes from believing I could make the change to or for the other person. I deluded myself by believing that something I could do would make a difference, make life easier or more manageable so the others would not have to drink or be depressed. I was helpful around the house. I tried to keep my siblings in order, keep the house clean, dinners made, clothes washed and tempers calm. I organized bills, washed cars, stayed away, stayed close, tried all extremes until I fell into my own disease. This was another extreme. Until then I had lived with the illusion that I could control or change my parents or their behavior. Pain came from disappointment time and time again. No matter what I did, I could not make them change.

Active addiction goes through a process of which the co-addict is quite aware: the stage of being wound up in the process of active use, the illusion of "fun," and the delusion that "this time it will be different." While on a spree or bender or toot, the addict is consumed with all of the other lies and promises of pleasure that lure addicts into actively engaging in their disease. Then comes remorse, physical sickness, guilt and shame. Now the addict is childlike, compliant, willing to do anything to restore them into the good graces of their para-addict. This is the moment for which the co-dependent lives. It seems as if all will be well and that a change will be made— they "really mean it this time." This is another second arrow: the co-dependent delusion.

Amanda Andruzzi wrote an entry in the addictionblog.com on May 9, 2013, that explains the many ways we shoot ourselves with the second arrow. We cover up (lie), we threaten (suggest harm), we bargain (stealing the truth), and we plead. We who suffer from second-hand addiction exhibit distinct codependent behaviors that are often presented as kindness and giving but are rooted in a need to control. None are successful, and their result is mental and spiritual agony.

Many co-addicts have a huge need to be needed. This was true for me. My desire to be helpful and useful has become overgrown—perhaps entangled in the illusion that I could help someone else into being other than they are. With a child, this helpfulness is appropriate at certain ages (tying the shoes for a toddler, for example), but we cripple our young children if we do not step away and allow them to struggle to learn this skill for themselves.

The person suffering from secondhand addiction also may thrive on being a giver—the generosities of helping, forgiveness and patience. This over-generosity can continue until you have given away your soul, denied yourself to the point that all you have left is resentment. In time, even the anger toward the other disappears, and nothing is left but self-doubt, depression and pain—all this in the name of "giving." This, too, is a second arrow. So, too, over-helpfulness toward an addict can in fact prevent addicts from finding their own limits on their addiction and climbing out of it. In fact, we may prevent them for becoming self-aware, self-empowered, and responsible for their own recovery. This over help-fulness can thus be a second arrow.

Another more insidious, hidden arrow—perhaps not initially pain-ful, but immensely uncomfortable when discovered—is this: hiding behind the addiction of another shields us from the need to look at ourselves. I found myself able to avoid looking at myself, my behaviors and my choices; they were always wrapped around "him" or "them." I put off learning how to make genuine give-and-take friendships, learn-ing how to disagree fairly, etc., by focusing on "other" rather than "self." I did this as a child—of necessity when I was growing up. I con-tinued this in my choice of friends as a teenager and in the choice of partners as I grew up. I was the martyr, the issues was always "theirs," and eventually it became a mantra for my drinking, as in, "You would drink too, if..."

It shocked, hurt and humbled me when I began to realize that as an adult I was in charge of that second arrow. I was saying "yes" to the untenable. I was behaving in entitled ways where no entitlement was due. I was abdicating responsibility for my life choices. And I was blam-ing others when my actions, attitudes and behaviors were mine. What a wake-up call. Compassionate recovery was needed, and I reached out to the sister programs of recovery to help me heal.

It was difficult for me to accept that these arrows are not exclusively from an open heart. In truth, by being wrapped up in the outcome of another's life, one can avoid one's own need for growth. When I am wrapped up in "him" or "her," I cannot see "me." The process of living with an active or relapsing addict has actually convoluted my coping mechanisms, so I, too, need to find a bottom and climb out. For this second arrow was my process of avoiding my own wonderful being. By remaining "other-focused" I could disengage from looking at myself, finding out my own needs, desires, boundaries, strengths and goals.

The huge and truly fearful unknown is *not slinging that second arrow*. Support and wise friendships are needed as a beginning to empty your quiver. It is a long road to recovery, and I falter at times. When I find myself sticking in a second arrow, I reach out to friends, I talk about it, and I look inward. What is this gripping serving? What am I avoiding in myself? I use kind words with myself: I look away from my object of temptation and say, "Dear heart—let go."

❧

July 19: Self-Love: Practicing the Principles in All of My Affairs

I recently took a workshop. Part of the process was to examine the self-created borders between others and myself. In this instance, borders are not boundaries—which are healthy and necessary. Borders are lines of demarcation. These can be judgments, prejudices, assumptions about others, assumptions about myself: "I am not wealthy, so I am not as good as those people," "I am not young, so I cannot relate to that group," "I am not flexible, so I can't do yoga," "He is wearing a hoodie and dark glasses, I should avoid him," etc. Borders can be overt, or they can lie just below consciousness. In order to find the limiting aspects in these borders, I have been using my yoga and recovery programs to *see* those borders, *see* myself, and *see* how these two entities interweave and stand apart.

Borders also add to my struggle to find the sweet, embraceable parts of my inner self. So how am I to find my inner worth, my goodness, my true values? The trick is not to let setbacks like borders floor me. I know I learn far more from my mistakes than my error-free actions. Knowing is in the head. The feelings can swing from "This is a learning opportunity" to "How can I be such a failure?" The former allows me to connect with people and with situations; the latter sets me apart from them. When I am in learning mode, I am connected to what I have done, heard or said, thus to the possibility of change and amendment. When I am hiding behind feelings of failure, or borders, I am wallowing in despair. I find my inner goodness by facing missteps with humor, grace and acceptance. Just that act alone, confronting my challenges, gives me a sense of dignity and satisfaction.

Self-defeating behavior and attitudes include looking at the wisdom and brightness of my students and giving into the concern that what I am offering is not "sufficient." I spend time with my teachers and mentors and think, "I will never get there" (wherever "there" is!). Those are all limiting beliefs that create borders between us—a group of "them" and a group of "me."

These false beliefs harken back to my work in the 6th and 7th Steps of my recovery programs. My shortcomings are characteristics born of an ego-deflation process that is an ego problem in reverse. Rather than the too-large ego—feeling exceptionally adept and competent—my too-small ego cuts me off, not just from others, but also from the yummy goodness inside myself. That veil of self-absorption is anathema to connection. Connection is crucial to remain in community with others, one's higher power, and one's true self. To reclaim community, I go back to the steps, the mat, the cushion and regroup, reframe, reconnect. Breathe. Take the deliciousness of my own experience, listen without judgment (of others *or* of self), integrate and inform my impressions without criticism, and enjoy the sweet, colorful salad of life.

This is the application of the principles in all my affairs. In the teaching and the learning, at home and on the road, in the classroom and the conference room, in the car and on the trail, listen with an open heart, and those unhealthy borders will change to healthy *bonds*.

⚬⚭⚬

October 21: Freedom as the Result of Boundaries: When Saying NO Means Saying YES

I am learning to have more healthy boundaries, which entails developing the skill to say NO. This is hard, for I risk displeasing others, and I risk that part of my ego that wants to be admired or regarded for always "being there," someone who will pick up the slack and other ego-feeding characteristics that actually have little to do with being of service. It also means I am standing up for my needs, myself, which seems—well, selfish.

Part of saying NO (thank you) is weathering the sting of turning someone down. I have a wonderful, replete life filled with people I love, care about, and want to spend time with. Saying NO sometimes means I am choosing to be away from them, choosing something else over being with them. This doesn't feel good, but I have learned to live with the discomfort, in part by choosing to say "no" to one thing to say YES to another.

I urge others to take time for themselves, to hold themselves sacred and dear. In fact, I lead self-care workshops and endorse all manners of boundary-setting as part of developing healthy self-respect and self-regard. I teach the skills I practice. I have self-care routines that can ground and prepare me for each day. I do these when they feel like work, and I do them as a discipline.

What I often neglect to do is to play. To take classes myself, to do something where I don't have a defined outcome or productive result. I do most things for a reason, and many things I do have an outcome: a meal, tidiness, a newsletter, an accounting report, a class taught, a conference call, a completed project, etc. But I have not taken time for the unreasonable in a long time. That would entail saying "no" to something already on my agenda. Who takes time for play?

The most playful thing I do is to play with clay, as a potter. *Clay-play.* To make space for this, I had to decline some wonderful friendship opportunities this past weekend, and to say no to other fun stuff, so I could sit down at the potter's wheel with a few pounds of clay and make something for no reason. I threw pieces that I crunched up and put back into the clay bag. I threw pieces that started out as one thing and became another. And the next day I followed up by trimming and decorating my creations. This was my first time at the wheel in over a year, but I needed to do this just for myself. Not to make things for sale or as a gift, not to explain or teach a pottery-making process—just for me. Open-ended time with no thought of result.

But after that first day of throwing; my body was out of whack, so I needed a yoga class for all reasons: physical, emotional, spiritual. And rather than lead myself in my own practice, I was willing, in the name of self-care, to lay my mat in front of another teacher and to be cared for.

By creating boundaries in my life, I was able to find freedom: freedom to play, freedom to create, and freedom to be a human *being*— rather than a human *doing*. The result of saying no was saying yes. I am refreshed.

⁂

December 28: Resolve to Love and Forgive

Many years ago I was on that treadmill of creating lists of things I would like to do differently in the New Year. Evidently I had imagined some magical difference in my ability to control my eating, spending, or what have you after midnight December 31. So the obligatory list would be made, gym memberships would be purchased, the requested workout clothes received as Christmas gifts would be laid out and ready for my body-toning enterprises. I was ready-set-go for the first run out the door on January First.

Planning to eat for health in the future, I consumed the last of the holiday cookies and chocolates while I selected recipes for the New Year out of magazines and newspapers, as the food columns had taken a lean turn after the indulgences of Thanksgiving and other holiday offerings. Other times, suffering from a debt hangover from holiday spending, I would make a resolution to be thriftier. Promising to live within my budget, I reviewed ads for post-holiday sale bargains. Watching people bike and run in the brisk winter air during the holidays reminded me of how I had let these activities go, and I made plans to dust off the sport shoes and start a walking regimen the next day.

But after years of disappointments and broken commitments, I dropped the resolution process altogether. I was tired of falling short of expectations and being part of the joke resolutions have become. Also, the things I truly wish to resolve, or continue to practice, have little to do with money, weight, or the physical trappings of life. My resolutions are balanced between "One Day at a Time" and setting intentions for living (a decidedly future-looking activity). They are balanced between my current step and the path before me. I make resolutions *daily*; not just on 12/31. The *sankalpa*, or resolution, is of an enduring nature, a quality I struggle with but wish to enhance and encourage in myself.

Rather than look at what I may want to accomplish, I am looking at how I will get there. Today I will forgive myself for mistakes, leaving more room for the successes to flourish. Today I will take care of myself when I am not well, using the skills I have learned to promote healing in body, mind and spirit. Today I rejoice in the times I have taken healthy action. Today I will practice the discipline of follow-through *and* congratulate myself for tasks completed. Today I will love myself as I am before all that is to come, and I will love myself in spite of all that has come before. I am lovable. This is my year, day by day, to inhabit my very *being*.

January 16: Asset or Liability?
Which Influences My Actions?

Looking back at my life before recovery and my life early in recovery, I see what huge part my guilt and shame played in my selection of jobs and relationships. They influenced what kind of living situations I tolerated, and even how I approached my spending and my budget. My concept of how others would perceive me also influenced my financial decisions: I would spend lavishly on others while denying myself similar pleasures. Guilt and shame determined how I handled requests and requirements from my bosses, and how I responded to those of my family.

I thus felt unworthy, which augmented my desire to overhelp and overshare, and ultimately affected my choice of partners. Looking back, I see how this choice of partner played out; my days were filled with dread about not being worthy. Later in recovery I was fearful that he would condemn me for my past. I accepted bad treatment as my due for being a bad person.

Eventually I became aware of my overcompensation for my low self-esteem, acting as if I had to *pay* to be alive, to reimburse others for my existence on this planet. My needs and desires were of no consequence; what others thought they needed was more important. I opened myself to danger, pain and disregard with this attitude; the result was a cycle of mistreatment, apology, overhelping, and disregard once again.

This changed when I began to observe myself, my behavior and my choices. I noted that my choices had led to being treated with disrespect. I was not treating myself with respect, thereby teaching others that I needed none. Through recovery I began the process to change the behaviors that led others to treat me badly. I started to incorporate attitudes and actions that led to a greater sense of self-esteem. I practiced, adjusted, re-balanced, and practiced again. I learned to keep my own counsel and to avoid oversharing, explaining and defending. I developed the courage to create boundaries and learned to enforce them. I learned to say NO.

Fast-forward many years. I have worked with women in the recovery program and as a mentor in other areas. I recognize the desire to be everything to someone else, to do way more than expected, perhaps to the extent of running roughshod over my own needs and desires. In my job I have managed such people—people who move too fast and work too hard trying to overachieve and over-please. I have reviewed their work performance and felt the need to guide them away from their overwork. Why? Certainly a boss, a company, a supervisor might love the overachieving, goal-oriented employee who will take on more than they can possibly do. A company loves employees who will do the work of two people. But this isn't good in the long run. It does not lead to a balanced life, a balanced outlook, a healthy being. So I counseled the whole person at my job and sponsor the whole woman in my program.

I would joke that companies prefer to hire someone early in recovery because, like me, the leftover guilt from previous neurotic behavior was an amazing motivator to overwork, overdo, people-please, and not stand up for oneself. I am not alone in witnessing the power of negative self-worth. In a comic strip published January 13, 2014, Scott Adams' amazingly perceptive Dilbert pointed out the boss's perspective on low self-esteem. He prefers employees who choose the corporate vision over pay and have low self-esteem as a bonus. This is a painful and unfortunately realistic view of poor management: get the work for a song, and the most likely people to buy into it are those who don't feel good about themselves.

I am a woman in long-term recovery—from low self-esteem, much of the time. What has my experience with low self-esteem taught me? How has it influenced my decisions? Whether it has been a negotiation about home repair, a search for new employment, performance of my job duties, my friendships, or my contributions to any effort, I take a breath, pause, and then decide if the person, place, thing or activity is appropriate for me at this time. I also examine the source of this decision: Is it an impetuous reaction coming from my historical being? Or does it evolve from a considered response from my healthier self? On what criteria do I now base my choices?

It depends. Actions and activities may be and look the same: working late, providing support to another, accepting ups and downs in a relationship, etc. However, they can be sourced in drastically different motivations and intentions, as these examples show.

Working overtime: One person may be coming from a place of sheepish feelings based on guilt and shame, another from expressing their internal value of getting this unique project done. The outcome may be the same (working late), but the motivation is different in each case.

At work: Am I overworking? If so, why? Have I decided to work late because of my ethics and values? Am I building resentment because I am doing it for *them* and they don't appreciate it? Am I able to set boundaries and ask for guidance with workload priorities when the volume becomes too great? Can I just do my best and then let the rest go?

In negotiations: Do I worry too much about offending the other party to clearly state what I need and what I can pay? Do I have skillful language and ways to express my requirements and expectations?

In relationships: Do I remember that I have worth and that I "matter"? Are my choices based on a belief that this is the best I can hope for, rather than real love and mutual respect? Do I make non-verbalized "trades" of one aspect of acceptability for another unacceptable attribute? Am I able to tolerate the other person not being happy with me at all times, while living my life according to my own values and ethics? Have I internalized the three "C"s of Al-Anon (applicable to more than just addictions) that I didn't cause, can't control and can't cure another's behavior? Do I accept us both just as we are?

In friendships: Am I more comfortable giving than receiving? Am I happier providing support than asking for it? Is there a balance of activities, expressing preferences, and sharing?

Working the steps of recovery has helped me to distinguish assets from liabilities, and how to moderate and modulate my characteristics, so I can bring myself into equanimity in these and other scenarios. Yoga has also taught me to know whether my actions are coming from a healthy place when I pause and listen to my gut (one of yoga's somatic benefits). I feel right when my actions are right, when they come from an integrated place. It takes time to recognize healthy feelings, to act on them consistently, and to look at my attributes and ask: "Asset or Liability?"

⌘

January 29: JUST STOP IT!

That's right—come to a rest, put your pencil (keyboard, tablet, device, list, or other "have to do") down, breathe, then come back for a bit.

Going going going, doing doing doing, getting getting getting. I suffer from the disease of "more." Addiction of all types sprouts from the field of "never enough" and grows to "all and then some." This was true for me in active addiction and continues to move along the edges of my reality to lesser degrees now, in various ways. I know I am in "trouble" when I reach for "just one more" cookie, spoonful of something, forkful of another, hand of cards, silly YouTube video, etc. This process and instinct reminds of "just one more" drink, drug or pill—a behavior of the past, which indicates that I am out of balance, out of integrity with myself. It is the disease talking. It can be a signal that I am avoiding something—namely the here and now.

It is amazing how the concept of "just one more" creeps into the socially acceptable behavior as well as the neurotic. I can be as ill with my duties as I had been with drugs: "just one more" administrative task, chapter of a book I am reading, pose I am deconstructing, commitment to add to my calendar, class to add to my schedule, etc. These are examples of how I can become nearly obsessed with a responsibility or a job. Staying at a task beyond quenched thirst, satiated hunger, relieved tension, etc., is another form of excess. So whether I am doing too many useful things or too many harmful things—if to avoid my genuine feelings and issues—I am letting busy-ness shroud authenticity. More activity is less reality.

Life In Bite-Sized Morsels

When the practice of "more" slips into my norm, I have difficulty stepping back. I have found, however, that overdoing often results in illness, and getting sick results in the ultimate stepping back. At times the only way to stop pushing myself too hard, to slow down, is to *stop*. Yet stopping completely has risks and challenges of its own, including laziness and poor productivity, Just as important as looking at why I overdo is looking at how I can rest, let up, take a break without being a slacker or a piker.

I have battled certain negative responses to self-care when falling ill. My discussions with myself include: *Do I really feel under the weather? Should I push through, or throttle back? Why do I seem to need to crash to "just stop it"? Am I afraid of babying myself too much? Is this why I resist taking a rest? Am I a quitter?*

As a woman in recovery, even after many years I still equate feeling sick with feeling hung over, which was a condition of my own making: I drank and used so much I was poisoned, sick, and unable to follow through on promises, much less take care of basic needs. Now, feeling similarly ill and weak brings on historical sensations of guilt and shame. This requires a bit of self-talk to overcome, such as remembering when I did push through and keep going when possible in pre-recovery, and that my skills of disregarding my physical self, nausea, headache, bone-weariness, etc., were necessary at the time. Yet they are not wise for motoring through a cold or the flu. By disregarding my symptoms and trying to continue to function, I treat myself with indifference and neglect. This is not acting wisely in recovery: this is not good for self or others.

To learn the quality of sufficiency, I must learn the telltale signs of overdoing and the symptoms of self-neglect: the third cookie, the next order from the discount online store, the fifth video of cute cats befriending rodents, etc. These behaviors of distraction stray my attention from what yearns to be done: self-care and the discipline of a moderate life. It is time to *just stop it.*

April 13: The Hubris of (Imagined) Control

I've started to think in a multi-dimensional way about my desire to control others and to control outcomes. I am subject to the deluded practice of control from time to time, falling victim to the illusion I can alter "people, places, or things." And then I catch myself, realign, and redirect. I get *myself* under control.

I understand the illusory nature of control: there really is no way to control another person. You can limit their choices or create uncomfortable consequences for their actions, to urge people in a certain direction. You can try to persuade and influence them. But their decisions essentially remain their own, even if the relationship is equal, the power structure is even and there is mutual respect. If all things are not equal, the control factor can be huge and disabling.

We exert control in the unequal relationship of parenting our children. I did. I created consequences and outcomes, for a whole range of behaviors: "Eat your dinner, or no TV before bed." "Do your homework, or you can't go outside and play." And later-in-life consequences: "If you come home after curfew, you will surrender your phone/car keys/privileges." In reality, I haven't "controlled" my child; I have merely placed specific outcomes as the result of actions taken or not taken. Similarly, my employer has "controlling" limits of timeliness, job completion and condition on the job: if you don't comply, you lose your job, etc. It is a process of self-selection: comply, or accept the consequences. These repercussions are usually straightforward and clear.

The messy desire to control can come in subtle forms: in some extremes I want to direct the thoughts and behaviors of others. *I want you to think well of me. I want you to treat me in a certain way. I want you to call right away. I want you to like me. I want my job, but I want other people at my job to be different. I want to let my adult children be adult and independent, but I want them to be so in a certain way—or to do or choose a certain thing. I want, I want, I want.* This takes up space between my ears, doing nothing for my relationship or my desired outcomes.

Life In Bite-Sized Morsels

In evaluating my need to run the show, I have discovered a conflict between my wants and the values I have. I value independence, but I want compliance from others with my ideas, plans and timelines. When my actions stem from this need to direct others, I am not behaving well. My next concern is: what if the person complies with my suggestion or direction? For example, I might compel someone to do something right now, and that person's other responsibility goes undone, which may have downstream consequences of its own. This is where the fullness of the word "hubris" comes in—at the point where I don't see beyond my wants.

A three-dimensional image can explain how I perceive the effect of hubris: a row of dominos. Let's say I take over from my Higher Power, the universal spirit, and get what I want. I see only myself and the next domino (the thing or person I want to affect), but not all the dominoes that come after that. I don't see all the spokes that radiate out from the person I am "controlling, such as that person's life journey and ability to learn and grow from experiences. I am not aware of how that person's actions, skilled or unskilled, are supposed to unfold in the world. I don't see the people and situations affected by that person's behavior and choices. Were I to control the tipping of the next domino, I will have affected all of the following ones. I have in essence "taken responsibility" for so much more that I cannot know or see—but not really; for no matter what I think or choose, I am *not* in control; the battle itself is an illusion. I realize I am able to make choices, and so are others. Each of us selects whom we listen to and what we follow—sometimes in a healthy way, sometimes not. Take a deep breath here and accept the fallibility of being human and having delusions.

Acceptance is a huge step to freedom in making choices—freedom from the opinions of others, freedom from the pain of saying "no," and freedom to say "yes." And, by understanding that in reality I don't control and am not controlled, I can really find freedom.

Huge note: I am powerless over addictive substances and the consequent behaviors. I have no control over what my disease will do to me when I act and use. I have accepted that the consequences can be imprisonment, institutions or death, and so I choose not to use, because I see those consequences clearly. No illusion there.

❧

July 16: Staying On My Own Mat

I've been having a rough time of it for the last week or so. Some of my difficult feelings have come from a change in my focus. I am reevaluating how I spend my teaching time, writing time and service time. I am feeling an internal shift as I look at my ego-self to determine who is driving the train here—my spiritual self, or my outward-looking, other-directed "success" striving self? This investigation has caused me to feel out of balance. Lack of internal balance is a dangerous condition for many, for change can be a toppler! I teeter on the edge of an emotional relapse when my internal world is off kilter.

How do I get out of balance? Distrust, depression, dis-ease, disassociation, despair. I am off my internal game and out of synch with life. I don't trust how I feel or what I sense around me. My confusion turns to anger, the anger turns inward, and I feel depressed. I am not at ease anywhere or with anything. I sense no solution, no resolution, no peace. I am separate from everyone, my heart and mind is wrapped in cotton wool, and nothing gets in. I ultimately feel as if nothing will *ever* change—I will just have to learn to live with this loss of connection to self, with others and my spiritual bond.

What is going on with my "internal shift"? I need certainty, predictability, knowledge of what is going on. When things change, I am in the process of changing, which is supremely uncomfortable, as I don't know what my new internal landscape will be. Will it be a change in life direction, focus, passion or desire, or a softening of any of these? The process of change has caused me to be 'elsewhere.' I am not here in the moment. My thoughts are going to the past and wandering to the future. I am not yet clear about where I am. What seems to have happened is my perspective has changed. This was not intentional, as I wasn't ready to change my perspective, my outlook, myself. It evidently happened when I looked away and ceased conscious effort.

Yet, from experience, I know that once I adapt to the new reality, I adjust to it. I won't stay depressed, down or disconnected. I will find my way out. Finding my way out of these dark feelings, though, has little to do with outward referencing and so much to do with internal acceptance. I adapt to the shift, accept not knowing, and courageously face the unknown. As I begin to surface, I realign with my higher power, my ethics, my values, and remember I am not alone: when the tenderness abates, I reconnect with my peeps and find my way out.

What does staying on my own mat have to do with anything? Everything. Sadly, I have discovered that I look to other people's mats: yoga mats, work mats, household and family mats. I compare. When I compare myself to other people, their yoga practice or teaching, or their lives, I begin to feel unmoored from my own. I look, I yearn, I compare, and I envy. I become out of balance with my own existence. Whether it is a pose, strength or flexibility in yoga, or whether it is life achievement or "success," once the comparisons start, the dissatisfactions grow. And, for some reason, I am always on the short end in my mind; not graceful enough in my *asana*, not accomplished enough in my profession, not giving enough in my community, and on and on and on.

Staying on my own mat, living my life personally, completely and with love and compassion brings me to the present. Bringing the reference back to self helps me to find the right size of my own life and get back in synch with my own true nature—back in BaLaNcE. The unanchored feelings of being out of touch with myself dissipate and become grounded in my own true nature when the focus comes back to my being and my calling. The internal shifts can settle, and I can face life with equanimity once again.

August 11: Good Fences Make Good Neighbors: Al-Anon and Yoga

I remember that quote, "Good fences make good neighbors" from Robert Frost's poem "Mending Wall." In high school we were asked to read and analyze this poem, and I did my best. I realize now that my understanding as a youth was pretty anemic and barely scratched the surface, as my life experience allowed for only the most superficial of understandings.

This poem, like his others, is complex and deep. It took a little recovery for me to get it, but luckily the early exposure had kept the stanzas in my head for later evaluation. In school, young and literal, with little self-knowledge or life experience, I had no idea why the teacher was so excited about this poem. *Wall, no wall, what's the difference? It is a low stone wall, a mere sketch of separation. It falls down easily in hard weather and is restored by informal agreement by the neighbors to its precarious state in the spring.* I did not understand the wall's true symbolic significance. It was merely a story.

I muse about the lines now, several decades later, and I wonder as Frost did, what are we "walling in or walling out"? There is nothing observable about an emotional wall, and yet we repair and maintain it to keep a semblance of demarcation between us. The wall can define boundaries, but it can also protect us from others. By developing this understanding, we learn what the wall really is: real, symbolic, emotional, *social*.

I look at a wall as a symbol for personal boundaries, and think about all aspects of it: both sides, you and me, inside v. outside. In the context of personal boundaries and "to whom I was like to give offense" (in Frost's words), I have learned to include myself in that review: I have a right to a wall, a right to my side. By removing a wall, I could put myself in an unsafe position. I may need to have a wall to keep another out and to keep myself safely in. The wall may be useful, or it could be created out of fear, insecurity, greed. Before I tear it down, I should know.

Trimming shrubbery in my yard, I came up close to the fence separating the neighbor's yard from mine, and Frost's poem popped into my head. This fence once was a low iron railing that was more decorative than confining. The elderly neighbor and I would stand across this tracery of iron and chat. She passed away, the house was sold, and a new, tall 'privacy fence' was built in the railing's place. I no longer know my neighbor. Pulling weeds, I muse on that.

Pondering about boundaries and how I need them in relationships, in defining what is my business and what is not. Having a clear sense of self, honoring and maintaining the actions associated with being a separate human being is important. It also teeters in confusion when I think about being part of the universal whole. How do I balance the benefit of being of service with risk of meddling, being helpful without being invasive? Functioning as a part of the universal whole, however, does not necessarily mean your business is mine.

We can have our limits and our borders. We can have the private and the public. The wall does not have to be large, wide, or in complete repair. When we honor it, the idea is enough. There is a healthy sense of self that is important to acknowledge and a healthy sense of *you* that *is* acknowledged; the wall is reassuring, the wall is a reminder that, even though "something there is that doesn't like a wall," we and our neighbors maintain it together, "and on a day we meet to walk the line," setting it up mutually once again.

If I know where you stand and you know where I stand, is it not more comforting? When my edges are blurred and meld, move and become dependent upon yours, the fences down, confusion and unhealthy interrelations can occur. The wall is necessary until its purpose is understood. Once understood, it can be considered useful or not useful. Its use must first be known. Then a choice can be made: to keep it in repair, or to let it crumble away.

My mat, your mat, my practice, your practice, my side of the street, your side of the street, the manifestation of my ethics and your practice of yours—all are separate. Impact is mutual; expression is unique.

The full poem can be found here: http://www.poets.org/poetsorg/poem/mending-wall

DEPRESSION, MOURNING AND HEALING:
Both Sides of Disabling Emotions,
Going In and Coming Out

I AM NOT immune. I am not immune to the pain of the unexpected, to the impact of the transitory nature of life and relationships, to the overwhelming experience of being. I am not above or beyond the feelings that can trip one up. I am not over or beyond getting hurt, being sad, feeling as if life were useless or I am useless or "things" are useless. I merely have more tools with which to pick myself up, talk myself through, and witness despair, sadness and other things that change.

Years have gone by in which I have shed not a tear—maybe a little moistening of the eyes, but only for the most sentimental of reasons: a movie, the motto on a card, or an ad. But the tears of pain at the time of the hurt, the tears of loss at the time of the death, weeping in a hospital or at a memorial don't happen for stretches of time. My heart clutches, my chest aches, my throat becomes tight and sore, but I don't cry. No boo-hoos for me...until that changes.

I have worried that I have a hard heart, that I have no deep feelings, that I have become calcified from my past experiences, the layers of unspent tears having become a shell preventing other tears from coming. I remember that I do have a tender heart. I am a compassionate person with both sympathy and empathy for others. Yet I get to a certain point in my feelings about my own pain and it just doesn't get to my eyes.

I was present at the death of both of my parents. As the eldest and most responsible child in my family of origin, many of the emotions were put on hold as the details were attended to. In the death of my father, I was my mom's support, taking care of logistics, organization, memorials and memories in a swift, efficient manner. I, as I had most of my life, tried to shield and protect Mom as I handled as many of the details as I could. Later, when she passed, I was in much the same position as I navigated the emptying of her house and furnishings, handling the bills and legal issues, and selling her house...all without a tear, as a motor-woman moving through what had to be done. Weakness? Yes! Sadness? Overwhelming at times, but overall nothing I couldn't push down to push through. It scared me.

In the past few years I have seen dear, kind people in my circle of friends die. A few were older; all died too soon. I lost two sponsors and eight friends. For some, I was witness to their suffering and illness and kept company with them as they moved down the road to their final breaths. Others I had seen off and on over the years, and at their passing I thought, *I wish I had gone to visit more often.* Yet others I had seen weekly, and then not so often, and then no more. Each time, the quality of loss filled my chest, my recollections of them and about them became more brilliant, and each thought became more precious. Such is the character of loss: memories become treasures.

Possibly due to so many passings, or to my phase and age in life, depression grabs me up in deeper, more unpredictable ways. I am trudging down life's happy road, addressing challenges as they arise, meeting opportunity with vigor, if not enthusiasm, and then, in one fell swoop, the rug is pulled out from under me, and I am devastated. There is no center, no stuffing, no edges. I feel as if I am coming apart, my insides are void, and the container of my being has lost its walls. Nothing matters, yet everything is overwhelming. I know about the tools, the Steps, the meetings and the phone. I know about counseling, talking to friends, and being kind. I have head-knowledge, but my feelings, my heart, aren't in it. Knowing isn't enough.

I have been around long enough to know that things change. That is the only touchstone for me as I try to get through the days—and it does last days. I feel awful, isolated, alienated from others. I know my medicine is to connect with others, yet I am unable to articulate my condition. At times I feel out of my body. Sleep eludes me, yet I can barely move.

Life In Bite-Sized Morsels

I can't make decisions, and I am inconsolable. I have an appetite, but nothing tastes good or satisfies me. There is no satisfaction of any kind. I just need to be in the presence of another person, to let the feelings move and pass through me—no suggestions or advice, just company. Providing witness to another without trying to fix, alter or control that person is a hugely difficult thing to do, and it is what I need. Yet I don't know how to ask for it.

Days go by. Things shift. I come out of it, but not before I get to the point where I wonder what the point of it all is, what is the reason for being: for being here, for working or not working, for talking or not talking, for being with others or being alone. My heart is vacant. And then it isn't. I don't know what happens. I can't say it was a good night's sleep or a healthy breakfast. It may or may not have been that meeting, that commitment met, or that person who called. All I know is, I have felt helplessly despondent many times…but I don't feel that way now. It changed. But in the midst of it—it is interminable, and I am alone.

Change from the condition of depression is good. All change is ultimately good, but frequently not enjoyed. I love predictability. I like to know what is going to happen next. Having a plan and having it unfold according to plan is a source of satisfaction. I feel uneasy with the unknown. Life is filled with the unfamiliar and unpredictable. When things veer off course and I am not emotionally in balance or secure, I can be deeply shaken. On occasion I am grounded and secure in my being and have an open relationship with the outcome of events. At these times change is not as alarming or disruptive—just different than expected. It is neutral.

Change is expected in some life circumstances: children grow up and people age. I age. My response to these known transitions can be accepting, but it can also be one of surprise. I knew my kids were going to grow up—just not *that* way. I didn't know how they would navigate the world as adults, what choices they would make, how little my dreams matter, should matter, could matter in their lives. No matter—I love the lives they have chosen, their decisions suiting them so much better than my ideas would. This is change—change over which I have no control.

DEPRESSION, MOURNING AND HEALING: Both Sides...

I knew I would get old, but I didn't realize what that would mean. I had no idea what effect aging would have on my self-image, abilities, energy and interests. I didn't realize the wrapping would become such a lie about the interior. My ideas don't match my energy, my body doesn't match my self-image, and physical discomfort often exceeds my desire for activity. We adjust to a lot as we age. There is a split between what I feel like and what I look like. Society and I do not agree on what an aging woman looks like and how she operates. This change brings another lesson in humility and who I really am.

There was such a brief time where the inside and the outside matched. Certainly as a young girl I felt I was always out of sorts with my environment, family and friends. As many people in meetings proclaim, I felt as though I didn't belong. Others had the top to the puzzle box, knew what the picture of life should look like, maybe even already had all of the edge pieces picked out. I had pieces. That was all—just pieces. I was an alien everywhere I was. As a young woman, deep in my disease of addiction, the inside and the outside were always at odds. Drinking and using brought them a little closer in synch for a brief period of time, but mostly this synchronization was further disconnection.

A decade of recovery brought amazing changes in both my interior and exterior selves. I had gotten healthy, gained confidence, regained my ability to learn, and acquired a new career. My self-care had improved, and I was emotionally, physically and spiritually integrated (most of the time). I looked better in my forties than I had at any other time in my life. It was physical, as my health and self-care had returned, but it was my interior shine and delight in life that really brought me a type of beauty I enjoy. I was integrated. For the first time, I felt that my insides reflected my outsides.

Yet time changes us. Now the wrapping—the physical—no longer represents the inside. Yoga helps a lot. I see the interior as the true representation of my being. I let my actions inform others about who and how I am. I inhabit this inside space with such passion I am at times surprised to see my reflection in a window, in a mirror, and hardly recognize the older woman who looks back at me. When I am fully connected to my real self, my higher power, and my purpose, this reflection does not bother me. I embrace and accept the change. But there are times when I do not. When I resist or complain, I realize that something is awry in my body, mind or spirit, recoiling from reality: that the privilege of being on this planet for a longish period of time is that I will age. I will change. Accept this, and the pain lessens, the disappointment abates, and I return to my true self.

Returning to my true self, reintegration, and healing have been critical to my recovery, the bedrock of my relapse prevention, and the condition of being I crave now, much more than the drugs, alcohol, sex and other addictions to which I had succumbed. Healing is not linear for me, nor has it been constant or consistent. There is a lot of "three steps forward and two steps back." I really work on accepting that as the pattern—a bit forward and a little less backward—and avoid the feeling that every back step is a backslide, never to be recovered from again.

Healing takes a long time. There are levels, reactions to the changes, and re-stabilizations after adjustments. The first time I went through the 12 Steps, I did it with the eyes of a woman who was newly sober but not yet well. I was still imagining that my actions and behaviors had hurt only a few in only the most superficial ways. I knew I had also victimized myself, but I wasn't really sure how, nor how that would play out in my life, affecting my relationships and choices in the near term. Then I got better. My glasses were less fogged, and my understanding about the effects of my own addiction on myself and on others, as well as the consequences of having been raised in a less-than-healthy home. I needed to do the Steps again. This time I was a little more discerning about my drinking-and-using career, and I had a little more to review about my actions and attitudes in early recovery. I was not instantly well when I walked into the recovery meeting rooms, and I didn't know what I didn't know. I now say, *I had become too healthy to be that sick anymore.* Another layer of healing had to occur.

Time passed. With the assistance of my therapist, my sponsors, the rooms (with the guidance of my connection with the universal spirit), and my own diligent effort, I was getting better, less influenced by the instincts of my addictive self, more able to recognize those impulses no matter where or how they would show up in my life. It finally seemed as if all were well.

Then I hit a wall. I had done all my conscious brain could do. I had investigated my thoughts and worked them through as best I could. Feelings were either blocked or welling up from nowhere in a most inconvenient way. I needed to do more work. But I needed new tools.

Yoga was the new skill to add to my recovery repertoire as mindful movement without goal. Exercise had been attractive, but its goals of weight loss, strength, distance or other measure became the focus, not the integration of body, mind and spirit. By contrast, yoga incorporated introspection, sensate movement, breath, and present-time awareness. And it broke me open. I felt feelings in a safe way with tools to knit myself back together—all in a single practice. I was using my body to get into my feelings and using my breath to heal my nervous system. I had found the holistic therapy for my holistic disease.

I am still growing. I am still healing. More is still revealed to me even today, many years into my recovery. It is painful. It is a blessing. I am delighted to be alive, to be flourishing, developing, reintegrating with my purest authentic self amid an ever-changing life.

⊷⊶

May 17: Losses and Pain to the Heart

My heart hurts. Tomorrow I go to the memorial service for a strong, indefatigable woman who knew how to enjoy life. She lived fully, edge to edge, even in the toughest times. She had challenges of all types, and she felt them. One of her gifts was in sharing the good times and the bad times, as they occurred, in the moment. She drew on the past as a measure of change, not as a place to languish. She neither hoarded the delights of the past nor wallowed in its difficulties.

She knitted as a hobby. She loved the color and feel of yarn, but she didn't like patterns so much. Avoiding them, she made scarves, hats, and neck-warmers, items to "free-style" and make without caution. She participated in a couple of art shows with me; the first year, she sold dozens of her pieces to her delight. I bought a few myself, and I will treasure them even more now.

As happens with the death of a member of my fellowship, so many of us gather to acknowledge the person who has passed. We comment on her contribution, friendship and strength. We who attend get to see the wide variety of lives touched and the numerous people who will miss her. I was able to celebrate achievements and mourn her passing with many others, but this is a loss I will have to process alone.

My heart was still in pain from a memorial a few weekends prior. Another dear friend had died. He was a support and a resource for me and my family—particularly my mom, when she was frail and I was out of town. He would check on her and her house, making sure all was well. His devoted attention brought us all comfort. His service went beyond looking in on my mom and helping countless men in AA. He took his care to people all over the world. He went with Lions Clubs International to distribute glasses to underserved people in rural areas of Mexico. Yet he was not noisy about this service; few others were aware of how he brought sight and insight to the "underserved" areas of people's lives.

He was also an avid golfer, and had a great sense of humor, which for many duffers is a critical element for enjoyment of the game. He was devoted to golf and allowed himself to enjoy every minute of it. He played long after he was able to walk the course. His friends helped him into and out of the cart when he played. And later he just went along for the ride.

My heart also hurt from the passing of a third friend four months prior—a motorcycle lover, and yet a complete gentleman. He welcomed everyone to the rooms of recovery and spoke often about what he learned from the women in the program: respect, kindness, and self-expression. He always had a good heart, and became more tender and loving as time went on. The gift of his reunion with his children was a story of hope for so many. While he looked rough and tough in his leathers, he couldn't have been more kind and giving—another example of how the wrapping—the physical—does not represent the inside!

And he was a pie aficionado. A favorite run for him and his motorcycle ilk was to a pie shop in a nearby town. This stopping place offered community, conversation, and all manners of pies. This was his trademark destination, and for his memorial he wanted pie for one and all—dancing and pies. And that is what we had.

He was kind to people in pain, welcoming to those who were uncertain and new. He was a family man who loved his kids. He shared his feelings and was not shy about that—a fine example of what it is to be a man. And now he is gone.

A friend from my teens, a woman I had loved and with whom I had also had some of my major fallings-out, has also passed. When I was broken down from using and drinking, living in another state, she came to get me. Flying out, she drove home with me. Through rain, sleet and fog we navigated our way back to San Francisco. This was a tremendously kind thing for her to do for me. I was five months pregnant, emotionally spent, physically ill, and unwillingly separated from my firstborn child, but she listened to me for 24 hours as we made our way to California. Later, we would drink and use together. Still later, she would stop. In fact, she took me to my first AA meeting, which was with the Gay Atheist Agnostic group on Geary Street in San Francisco.

She was a spunky, wild risk taker. Her life was not lived according to any conventional standards, on neither a personal nor a professional level. She was a deep, humorous writer who told tales about herself, her family and her encounters. Her works were compiled into a book and published posthumously. ("Sirenita Lake", Chris Gutierrez, Heat Seeking Publishing, 2013)

At her life celebration, which followed a drum-and-song parade from the church where the service was held, there was an amazing number of people she had touched, standing to share their stories of reprieve and restoration. She was my age, she is gone, and she is missed.

Those were not the only losses. Soon my father-in-law, other friends, and my sponsor would leave us. Beacons of light and understanding have gone out in the physical world, but remain here in my tender heart, which hurts just a little right now but is grateful to have known them all.

❧

June 14: "It's All In Your Head"

Some of us have heard our whole lives, "It's all in your head," meaning that whatever we were feeling was an illusion or delusional thought. We had no reason to feel that way. The implication was that we were not in reality, and our responses and reactions were based on...nothing. The true fact was that we were responding (with more or less skill) to what was going on around us—sometimes said, sometimes unsaid, but we felt what was going on. Our brains were telling us the truth. We may have been powerless or incapable of responding in a healthy way, or at all. But it was in our head, and it was reality.

As a child of an alcoholic, I learned well how to gauge my environment. I developed coping mechanisms based solely upon the criteria of staying safe. These included an ability to feel the type of energy in a room—angry, calm, anxious, etc. These feelings pulsed through my nervous system and ended up in my brain. What I felt and thought was based on what I intuited and saw, but the adults around me disavowed my reality. When I expressed myself and heard that phrase, "It's all in your head," I became frightened. It scared me away from believing my mind.

Imagine my delight when I discovered they were right! It was in my head! I was feeling and perceiving danger, fear and insecurity correctly. It *was* all in my head and it was not an illusion; it was concrete reality. The traumas of a chaotic, unsettled household and my later active addiction had, indeed, changed my brain. The chemistry in my brain was certainly affected by ingested drugs and alcohol, but more important is that my lifelong experiences had changed the functioning of my brain. What I had endured as a child had actual physical effect on my nervous system and the makeup of my brain.

But the good news is: just as sensory inputs had harmed the brain, wise, healing sensory inputs can restore it. Yes, the brain can be healed! The thinning of the cerebral cortex and the overactivation of the amygdala and hippocampus can be reversed. The overactive nervous and hormonal systems that result in the processing of all manner of disappointments as threats and traumas can be healed and calmed. Realizing that trauma exists at other levels as well—in the body and in the sense of self—finding healing modalities that can address these areas is important. Integration of body, mind and spirit can effect the most resilient, long-term healing.

Research indicates that meditation and breath practices can rewire the brain along positive neural pathways. Changing our self-talk furthers this repair. The brain is a lot more plastic than previously thought; even traumatic brain injury has a longer, more positive trajectory of repair than the two to three years postulated just a few short decades ago.

The tools we can use to restore us to health and balance are simple, but require dedication and discipline to yield long-term positive results. With breath, meditation and mindful awareness, as well as intentional movement, damaged brain centers can be brought back online. The hemispheres can reestablish a relationship: right-brain and left-brain can reunite. You can re-integrate the "dis"-integration of the brain, your being and your sense of self. Yoga combines these three modalities, which is why its effects are so tremendous. A brief, consistent practice over a relatively short period of time shows results: the trauma that turned off functioning in the brain can be repaired.

How yoga does this is unique. As a practice, it can release tensions and traumas locked in the body. Our muscles have knots; we all have felt them. We also have deeper areas of tightness and tautness that can impair our mobility, add to chronic pain, and even create areas of physical blindness, areas we no longer claim or "see" with our proprioception. A result of injury, accident, surgery or other events dulls our ability to sense parts of our body, connections and muscles.. Releasing tightness in these areas with mindful movement, breath and kindness can allow the brain to come back "on line" and recognize these areas. The brain can heal, and the stories of past traumas can be let go.

So it *is* in your head—and that is the good news. What you feel and sense are real. The degree of reaction and sensation may not come from present time, but from unexpressed, held feelings and past responses. Trust yourself. Not all thoughts and feelings are subject to expression, but they are subject to being recognized, and even honored. Once the burden of the past is released, responses to current time feelings become more "right-sized," and the actions taken, and words spoken become moderate and considered rather than dramatic and disproportionate. Take time to breathe, meditate, and move. Reintegration is a powerful force for relapse prevention.

❧

June 24: Habits, Addiction and Brain Changes

The brain is an amazing organ. I know you don't need me to tell you that; you may have witnessed it yourself, the memories you have, the solutions you can find, as well at the wit and creativity that are part of you. These all influence the pattern of your neural connections and the way your brain operates.

I love reading about neuroscience. I am not a good "rememberer," so I have to repeat my readings over and over. Yet with each review I retain more and can integrate knowledge from one source to another. By learning about the negative brain changes from addictions, hearing about the intellectual and emotional recovery that occurs in 12-Step groups, and reading about other people's journeys in books, I am able to correlate and incorporate what I have learned.

A news article posted June 20, 2013, in *The Guardian UK* discussed uses of brain-imaging technology. Using an amazing combination of computing and image analysis, scientists have created a detailed 3D image of a brain that can be viewed from all angles and depths. This technology can determine where and how the brain is stimulated when certain senses are invigorated, which can lead to greater understanding about what goes on in our cranium during craving and active addiction.

This 3D brain-imaging also enables us to view the brain in the grips of a disease using color scans. We also know that using substances and/ or participating in addictive behaviors changes the neurological reward patterns in the brain, as well as hormonal balance and the emotional patterning that responds to the hormones. I was surprised to learn that the brain changes from addictive behaviors are very similar to those from substance abuse. That sounds about right—I was an all-purpose addict, changing easily from sex to alcohol to drugs to food, all the while suffering from unhealthy relationship addictions. Many of us have experienced the substitution of one addiction for another: stop smoking, start eating; stop drinking, start buying things; cease drugs, begin online gaming, etc. The brain is loath to give up the stimulation circuitry. Our neurons need to fire in the ways they are accustomed to firing, but they don't fire without that activation. These 3D images show that negative behavior alters the brain, which had retained the actions as neurological patterns.

I am excited about the science and the visual tools we have now that document what the ancients have known for thousands of years. Yogis call this *samskara,* or "the habits of the brain." We have *samskara* around belief systems, punishment and reward systems, expectation and disappointments, and so on. Over and over we replay and reproduce these mental customs as they are familiar—not because they are healthy or good, but because we are used to them. The more often we replay them, the stronger they become. The yogis of old knew this, and have teachings to alert us to the nature of the *samskara* and lessons on how to re-route these beliefs, assumptions and behaviors.

I have been reading *Some Assembly Required: A Balanced Approach to Recovery from Addiction and Chronic Pain* by Dan Mager, MSW (CRP 2013). The whole book is filled with "ah-ha" nuggets, but on the subject of *samskara* Mager relates the tale of the wheelbarrow on a dirt path.

Pushing a wheelbarrow along a path creates a groove on it. The more frequently the barrow is pushed along inside this furrow, the deeper the furrow becomes: "There comes a tipping point where it becomes harder to get the wheelbarrow out of the rut than to continue to follow it, which makes it only deeper still." (p. 63)

Now we know this from a scientific perspective: *habits of any type change the brain.* We rely on this phenomenon to assist with learning of any type, from the simple, such as brushing teeth, walking, identifying letters and reading, to the more complex, such as spatial relationships/ map reading, information relating to the operation of tools and cars, and aspects of our professions and careers. The brain creates pathways so we don't have to think about these things anew each time we do them. "What fires together, wires together" describes this most clearly.

Unfortunately, this also happens with the habit of reaching for the third cookie when we *said* we wouldn't. It happens when we play "just one more" hand of cards, purchase one more outfit, or take a pill just "one more time." We develop a habit of "not listening" to our wisdom mind, to our ethics, to our sense of "knowing better." Our automatic response to a familiar stimulus or temptation becomes perfunctory, whether we want it to or not. To give an analogy: Get into an automatic transmission vehicle after driving a standard for some time, and you will find your foot reaching for the clutch, as the situation of coming to a stop sign keys the *automatic response* of down-shifting. Which might not be so bad, but if we are stuck in traffic and habitually respond to that situation with anger over delays on the road, each time we are presented with a similar circumstance we respond with the vigor of the initial anger. Warranted or not, anger at delay has become a conditioned, habitual, automatic response.

The solution is to create positive habits of the mind, to slowly replace negative thoughts with positive ones, to carefully practice changing the course of your *samskara* with discipline, support, and courage—in time, perhaps avoiding it altogether. It takes vigilance and diligence to create new furrows, to foster new mind patterns, to restore healthy balance to that beautiful organ, the brain. Once you notice the rut, reach out for healthy companionship, wise counsel and support to help you define new paths and avoid the old. Be patient as your brain heals and rewires itself. It takes time. With care, you will flourish anew.

⌘

October 19: Loss, Service and Gratitude

Recently I had a bit of a wait at the San Jose International Airport. I was chatting with a woman in the sitting space near the boarding area, striking up conversation with a stranger as one can do in these situations of mutual "pause." She was also on her way to Maryland. She was going to the annual National Fallen Firefighters Memorial weekend, which she does annually to support the spouses of other firefighters who have died in the line of duty. She was lovely. As a widow, she could empathize; as a survivor of loss, she could offer guidance and hope.

Boarding was finally called. We got into our lines and headed onto the plane. I gave it not another thought as I got settled. Upon arrival in Maryland, I headed to my accommodations and plunged into the preparations for the S.O.A.R.™ training. I sussed out the building where my classes would be held, straightened the presentation room, located nearby lunch places for the students, and ensured that we had sufficient handouts and that I knew how to use the video equipment. Involved in the administrative aspects of putting on a training, all thoughts of firefighters left my mind.

Teachers and trainers, healers and helpers, we all met at the S.O.A.R.™ training to improve our ability to serve ourselves, our students and our families. Every person attending was there in the spirit of generosity—to give cleanly, clearly and openly to others their experience, strength and hope from both recovery and yogic perspectives. The training involved sharing some difficult events from one's past, both the tolls and successes of transition and transformation.

The depth and honesty of the intimate sharing, combined with the strength of the attendees, filled me with hope and gratitude. They returned home, leaving with me a wealth of input, serenity, strength and opportunities for growth. With the enthusiasm for the work we do, we are all better for having met one another. We all participated, playing with one another; bringing personal attributes like strong stones in building the foundation of a community.

Boarding an airport shuttle for my return trip, I met three open, friendly, and vibrant young men who had also been to the National Fallen Firefighter's Memorial—an amazing coincidence. They were also part of the fallen firefighter community, and their participation in the event, like that of the gutsy women I had talked with at the airport, gave it strength and healing power.

My mind draws lines and relationships between events—the markers or signs that inform me on my journey. It was no accident that I met the woman (widowed since 1999) on my way out to Maryland and then these three firefighters from Utah on my way back. These people found strength in being of service and in their lives, even after the loss of loved ones. They shared their experience, strength and hope with one another, each story giving courage to others who were newly on that path. Thus there was a parallel between their lives and mine. All those who attended the S.O.A.R.(™) training in Maryland with me had been through some annealing flames in life—fires of the spirit, of relationships, of challenge, of disease, and of death. We, too, could emerge from loss and pain with gratitude and in service. In coming together as a group, we could also inspire courage and change in each other.

⌘

November 29: Calm Can Cause Discomfort

At times calm can cause anxiety. When I am in the tornado of always doing, I can become uncomfortable taking a pause, taking a break, finding rest. In the throes of being out of balance, hungry, angry, lonely or tired, I am nearly resistant to disengaging, letting go and quieting down. Certainly at this time meditating can make me itch. My background as an adult child of an alcoholic reinforced in me a basic distrust of calm and peace. This behavior of being relaxed and calm needed to be learned. Not only when I am in the throes of HALT (Hungry, Angry, Lonely, Tired), but also when I am coming down with an illness do I find this newer behavior of harmony and calm elusive, yet all the more necessary. When I cannot tolerate peace, I need it most. Anxiety is the flag, the caution light, the klaxon of urgency: let go, take a break, pause. I see it easily in others; I am slower to know it in myself.

Students are often most restless in *savasana*, the final pose of a yoga practice. Reclining in tranquility pose after an hour of activity is sometimes more than the new student of yoga can tolerate—initially. The cessation of activity can cause nervousness and apprehension. In *savasana* the sequelae of feelings can erupt in tears, restlessness, and even laughter. The mat is a microcosm of life itself. Being overactive in life can prevent us from having to examine our feelings; at rest, they can burst forth. So I practice coming to a rest from time to time, when I am feeling strong. With practice I have been able to tolerate the effect of stillness, even when I have been on edge. It starts with the breath and continues through all types of letting go: contemplation, prayer, and meditation.

When life gets full, when I have been involved in a disagreement or a confrontation, when I have let the less-than-lovely parts of myself bloom and show, I make an effort to cease all activity, to breathe, and to feel. Stillness enables my feelings to freely move through me, make themselves known, express themselves in my consciousness, and move on.

⚭

July 7: Something Else, Not This, Not Now

Today was supremely painful. My soul hurt. My regular pattern was off. Dreams lingered without message, and the beginning of the day felt awkward. My yoga practice was OK, but did not transport me as it so often can. I reached out to find comfort, checking online for what my peeps were doing in the field of yoga and recovery, which normally lifts me up. My recovery friends share uplifting quotes and pictures of family and friends, and my yoga community inform all about what they are doing. I saw their posts of progress, of gratitude, of classes taken and classes given. Yet my heart hurt so much that all I saw was an example of what I was *not* doing. My ego was filling my eyes and blinding me. I saw their comments and accomplishments as a mockery of my own (or lack there-of.)

I watched myself be in pain, in discomfort, out of balance. I was not in my body. I said to myself, *this is me brushing my hair from my face. I am moving through the room. I am sitting. I am disintegrating.* This was not good for me. I yearned to be whole again.

I sent in the "second arrow"; not only did I have these feelings, but I criticized myself for them. I thought, *I shouldn't feel like this.* Deny the feelings? Not recommended, but it seemed to be part of my survival instinct. *If I keep the feelings at bay, maybe they won't overwhelm me. If I deny them, maybe they aren't true.* Comparing myself to others kept me alone. I created that boundary between them and me, isolated myself, and felt as if nothing and no one could help.

Hold me! Hold me UP! I felt like shouting "*Is anybody out there?*" as in the song. I turned on the radio—the station bothered me. I tried another—that was wrong, too. I turned it off. I picked up a book—no good. I reached for another—same thing. No food-fills. No song-thrills. *If everything seems wrong, I know it's me. Even knowing that is no help. I am usually so strong, the one who holds compassionate space, giving permission to another to express the true feelings of the moment...but not now! Now I need the support, and I don't know how to ask in a way that people will hear me. Being seen as strong prevents people from hearing my soft cries of desperation. Seeing myself as strong prevents me from shouting.*

Depression could lead to emotional relapse. This might be one of those times. I wasn't prepared for this. I know you often don't see depression coming. Even with hard times or special stresses, you don't know if or when you will be knocked off your feet. It came unannounced. It woke up with me today. It came out of the blue, making me blue. My vision was skewed. Joy for others appeared as sorrow for self. The poison of toxic thinking…I am not immune.

One foot in front of the other. This too shall pass. Reach out to others. Write. Cry. Then get to a meeting, even if it is a "lousy" one. Rinse and repeat. There was no secret answer as I whispered to myself, *Be where you are.*

I might be listening.

~

August 12: Not Waving but Drowning

In the wake of yet another death from the pain of life—Robin Williams—I posted a poem on Facebook that seems to have struck a chord with many. Here it is in full:

Not Waving but Drowning
By Stevie Smith (1902-1971)

Nobody heard him, the dead man,
But still he lay moaning:
I was much further out than you thought
And not waving but drowning.
Poor chap, he always loved larking
And now he's dead
It must have been too cold for him his heart gave way,
They said.
Oh, no no no, it was too cold always
(Still the dead one lay moaning)
I was much too far out all my life
And not waving but drowning.

Responses included:

"WOW. "Not waving but drowning."

"When you get too famous and too big—other people are afraid to come close, people seem to think you don't need much help and they stay away when you need them the most. Sad but true--" SP"

"This is a terrifying reality-not having support, from the outside looking in the picture, the life, the challenges and the graces are all so different from being inside the life feeling and living it. Too famous to ask for help? Yoga master teachers acting out and behaving badly, actors and singers feeling so out of synch with the public's impression of them that they lose their self knowing. Even being so big that you think the rules, society's conventions, ethics and morals don't apply to you as they do to mere mortals; this is all so painful. And then, illness strikes and the future is inordinately bleak. The prospect of needed to ask for help on a regular basis overwhelms your idea of the possible. When people retreat should you follow them? It is invasion of privacy to ask one more time 'Can I sit with you?' Witnessed sadness may not be as overwhelming. Sit on the beach; look at the water, don't go in."

"That poem is exactly what it feels like to someone suffering through severe depression. As one who suffers with this illness into a decade; One minute you're on the beach waving, and the next minute you are out to sea. When you're out to sea you have to pray there is someone on shore looking for you...in many cases it's easier to just let our depressed friends lapse from our memory..." SS

"One minute you're on the beach waving, and the next minute you are out to sea." There is no announcement "I am going down now" in a reasonable voice, in a way most people can hear. Rather than letting our depressed friends fade away, just listening is a huge gift—not solving, not commiserating, just letting them talk or letting them sit in silence. Let's look out for one another.

Depression coupled with addiction, or addiction as a response to depression, is toxic and sad, and can be fatal. Reach out. Get help. Find help. Be helpful. Ask for help. Make it clear you are not waving.

If you are unsure about how someone is doing, ask, wait a moment and ask again. We all say we are fine as a knee-jerk reaction to the question, "How are you?" Maybe we need to be asked twice. As SP said, sometimes the more famous, more competent or more collected one appears, the more difficult it is for that person to ask for help.

Call your friend and ask how you can be of help if you are unsure. Definitely call if you need help. Another person's voice and listening ear may be all that is needed.

About the Author

———— ⊂⊗⊃ ————

KYCZY HAWK IS the Author of the Central Recovery Press best selling book *"Yoga and the Twelve Step Path"* (2012). She has been in recovery since 1985 and has been an active yoga practitioner for the last ten years.

Kyczy teaches yoga to people at all stages in recovery, from all manner of addictions and co-addiction. This has given her opportunity to share her experience, strength and hope, as it has allowed her to learn amazing lessons from her students. Creating S.O.A.R.™, Success Over Addiction and Relapse, she has been able to teach other yoga instructors some key skills and techniques to teach in a trauma informed and somatic enhanced manner. This style has been developed to invite self acceptance and reconnection with body, mind and spirit.

Kyczy is also a certified Y12SR (Yoga of 12 Step Recovery) space holder. The Y12SR meetings she leads have been held since 2008- now entering their fifth year. These serve people from all recovery paths at all stages of recovery. Doctors and chemical dependency programs alike refer clients to join the group.

She teaches workshops and leads retreats using recovery and yoga principles to invite deeper self understand and compassion: key components to holistic recovery.

Kyczy lives in the San Francisco Bay Area with her husband Bill. She writes, practices and teaches yoga, and plays with clay when ever she can. Their children and grandchildren live in the Northern California area and they visit with them frequently.

Praise for "*Yoga and the Twelve Step Path*" (Central Recovery Press, 2012)

Publisher's Weekly 4/12/2012
"Her simple walk-through of the parts of a true yoga practice, which includes rules for behavior, physical exercise, and breath and meditation practices, make a basic yoga practice highly attainable."

Yoga Teacher Magazine (Vol 2 Issue1); Lisa Francesca (Author of "The Wedding Officiant's Guide: How to Write and Conduct a Perfect Ceremony.")
"Hawk's book restores the connection [to Eastern philosophy], and in fact builds a new and sturdy bridge for today's practitioner. While she provides some theoretical background, I found her book to be immensely and immediately practical. Her findings come from years of daily practice and self-study, and her tone is warm, clear, and compassionate."

Brenda Perlin, Author of "The Brooklyn and Bo Chronicles" and others
"This book offers so much good information and was very easy to follow. I like how it was written with honesty and went into great detail for the reader to understand the benefits of yoga in everyday life.
I can tell there was a ton of research that went into writing this book. It is very impressive and I would suggest it to all my friends."

Yogi Times; by Anne Heffron, teacher, writer and co-screenwriter of "Phantom Halo" released 2014
"This is the book that you will have next to your bed for the times when you feel invincible and want to deepen that strength and for the times when you feel frightened and helpless and need some tools to help you remember that along with the morning comes the light."

Om Exchange UK: Indira Kubachek writes that its is "an insightful and inspiring book based on personal experience that will guide addicts through the road to recovery."

Made in the USA
San Bernardino, CA
11 June 2015